T.S. Eliot
A Cross Cultural Perspective

T.S. Eliot
A Cross Cultural Perspective

Adibur Rahman

ATLANTIC
PUBLISHERS & DISTRIBUTORS (P) LTD

Published by
ATLANTIC
PUBLISHERS & DISTRIBUTORS (P) LTD
7/22, Ansari Road, Darya Ganj,
New Delhi-110002
Phones : +91-11-40775252, 23273880, 23275880, 23280451
Fax : +91-11-23285873
Web : www.atlanticbooks.com
E-mail : orders@atlanticbooks.com

Branch Office
5, Nallathambi Street, Wallajah Road,
Chennai-600002
Phones : +91-44-64611085, 32413319
E-mail : chennai@atlanticbooks.com

ISBN 978-81-269-1769-9

Printed in India at Glorious Printers, A-13, D.S.I.D.C.,
Jhilmil Industrial Area, Delhi-110095

Preface

The poetry Eliot explores, moves around the amalgamation of diverse identities. Eliot loves illustrating the un-illustrated. He takes up a single idea of the diverse identities and projects it at length in various stages of his poetic career. In other words, his discursive poetry, which he presents during his early and later poetic career, is an extended metaphor of loss of inheritance which defines itself in Eliot's usage of "a heap of broken images". The technique of objective correlative that Eliot applies doesn't merely mean putting restrain on the flamboyance of high voltage emotion, rather he camouflages his diverse experiences through it. Eliot is realistically conscious of both the primary and secondary imagination which seeks definition in the externalities of human behavior. Restraining the subjective feeling is just one aspect of the role played by the mechanics of objective correlative. Eliot was inescapably in need to restrain and cover up those subjective raw emotions and his coming across of discordant experiences which troubled and excited him intensely.

To Yeats, old age was a "mocking absurdity". He just made compromise with his ageing process which ultimately comes upon man expressing itself in terms of loss of vitality. Yeats found himself a great misfit in the modern age. The younger generation caught up into the web of sensual music finds expression in his Byzantium poems. W.B. Yeats, like T.S. Eliot, pathetically found himself seized up with the idea of frustration and despair. The larger did Yeats try to run away and escape from the ideas associated with reminiscences of Maud Gonne, the larger did he miserably fail in discarding ideas associated with her—the idea of frustration in love made her emerge in each and every line Yeats wrote. The primary imagination thus enabled Yeats to build up his poetic power. In many of Yeats' poems, ideas and reminiscences associated with Maud Gonne bypass and overtake his poetic sensibility. Yeats' heart goes wild and violent after the impulses of the mind get stirred up with her reminiscences. His imagination goes on to dwell not on the women won but on women lost too. Eliot in an identical way is a poet of pessimism and despair; he felt the pulsating beat of his subjective raw emotion which acted as an infrastructure for evolving a formula, a mechanism to restrain and camouflage all those diverse experiences incurred during his early and later stages of his life. Eliot's subjective raw emotion and his sojourn at Boston did not allow him to get divulged from those reminiscences coming upon his sensibility gathered at Boston and sought making inroads into his private workshop of poetry. The solipsistic technique applied by Eliot acts as inertia of the self; the whole transaction of seeking stance in the illusive realistic society depicted in his major poems like "The Wasteland", "The Hollow Men" and "Gerontion" move around the doctrine of the inertia of the self. Eliot's coming across of varied experiences incurred in both the American and British landscapes embroiled and excited his mind in such a way that the subjective raw emotion sought their definition in the fabric of his poetry. These emotions came so intensely on to the consciousness of Eliot that he found himself compelled enough to take them up and make them a part and parcel of his poetic creativity.

Grappling with his diverse experiences is thus the basic problem which essentially makes Eliot a poet of despair and pessimism. The subjective emotions according to Eliot thus seeks definition in the externalities of human behavior and need to be aesthetically ratiocinated. The yardstick of his usage of aesthetic verse hence comes to rescue Eliot from the hierarchy caused by those discursive, dissimilar and heterogeneous ideas and experiences so that art could be presented in all its true and purest forms. Thus, the basic reasons of applying the mechanics of objective correlative is not only to suspend those subjective feelings and intense passion, which he feels seek release in the behavioral patterns of man living in the modern Wasteland, he is also true to the mettle of his self as he avoids taking those subjective feelings incurred at various stages of his poetic career. Eliot is true to the mettle of his self in letter and spirit. He solipsistically believes in living with those discursive experiences and cumulative feelings—the sum totality of experiences; the sweet and bitter reminiscences that project the whole of Eliot. Eliot is 'honest' enough to present the varied assimilating experiences, the American and British, with a big heart which enable him to project the whole truth. The three witches in Shakespeare's *Macbeth* unfold a partial revelation of the truth. Eliot on the other hand, by intermingling both the American and British sensibilities, intends to project the whole gamut of assimilating discursive experiences incurred at length in terms of time and space, which is not a partial revelation of the truth, rather his poetry written at various levels of time and space, which presents the whole truth.

Eliot's major poems like the "Waste Land", "Hollow Men" and "Gerontion" are essentially an outcome of the decay of culture. He is equally influenced by Matthew Arnold's disinterestedness. As such, Eliot emphasizes the role of tradition in shaping up every existing generation. Arnold on the other hand projects his own canons of criticism based on religion and morality. Arnold defines criticism as a disinterested endeavour to hear and propagate what is best known in the world. The first principle of criticism Arnold formulates is disinterestedness which can be attained by keeping oneself aloof, what he attributes to a practical view of criticism. In Eliot's point of view, culture provides the basis on which art and literature need to be interpreted and understood. It can however be said that Eliot's decision to be naturalized as a British subject and to be anglicized by the anglican church, was part of his quest of the spiritual anchorage that could give sustenance to his cross-cultural foothold. His early poetry, on the one hand is reminiscent of Boston. In *Love Song of J. Alfred Prufrock* and *other poems*, the characters he portrays are ironically oblivious of their ethos, milieu, root and cultural heritage, and can be seen talking of Michaelangelo without being conscious of its meaning. His later poetry is reminiscent of Mississippi River and the Dry Salvages.

As Eliot was inspired by Matthew Arnold, he strikes a note of difference between culture and anarchy. Eliot's cultural outlook is twofold: first that assimilating cultures in the postmodern society give rise to ethnological confusion, secondly they are used for setting right the ethnological confusion caused by the prevalence of assimilating cultures. This becomes evident from his play, *The Cocktail Party*, in which he highlights the problem of assimilation of cultures and societies, and its consequences, effects and after-effects on the thought patterns of the modern society. In *The Family Reunion,* characters too emerge from the cross-cultural stock of society in which they interact, argue, look round and assert their cross-cultural identity. In *Tradition and Individual Talent*, Eliot himself makes confession of the basic fact how every generation has its own preference, proclivity and response to art, culture and society from the cross-cultural standpoint. Eliot thus gives a new meaning to correction and elucidation of taste. I.A. Richards reiterates that knowledge is power, but Eliot's approach to interpretation and analysis is different from that of Richards. Eliot is conscious of the form, pattern and shape of culture needed for the promotion of art, creativity, polish and refinement. In his significant essay, "Notes Towards the Definition of Culture", Eliot says that larger is the degree of culture, refinement, polish and decency, the larger would be the degree of perception, insight and creativity, which says he, contributes to rich heritage, ethos and tradition. To Eliot, culture and society are indispensable to each other. Art can't be studied without taking into account the rich heritage of culture and ethos. Too much knowledge as explained by Richards, says Eliot, hardly presents a meaningful form of art. Richards basks in glory with all possible meanings, shapes, forms of art, language and identities emanating from a work of art. Richards is liberal enough to go through the possible shades and subjects of meaning which act as an extended metaphor of the semantic principles. Unlike Richards,

Eliot applies his aesthetic principle in his private workshop of poetry. He applies his logistics, compares and contrasts; clips and curtails whatever is contrary to his concept of understanding and enjoyment; and goes for correction and elucidation of a work of art. James Joyce, in his works like *A Portrait of the Artist as a Young Man* and *Ulysses* applies his manifold experiences of guilt consciousness so that he could realize a larger identity. The usage of epiphany, the image of flow and images of flight help him liberate from the mundane world.

Eliot wrote a new kind of poetry. Its symbols, images and poetic devices are unconventional in their tone and tenor. The images like "smog", "a heap of broken images", "broken column", "stone" and "fire" point out how they are suggestive of the failure of realistic sensibility. The poetry Eliot wrote is more intellectual than emotional. The colossal growth of the realistic society and web of scientific facts says he, result in the phenomenal experiences like alienation and rootlessness. Richards on the other hand applies the verbal and structural interpretation done in a classroom reading. Eliot in his various stages of writing poetry at length, shows disillusionment with the realistic growth of society. The baffling experiences projected in his major poems are indicative of the basic facts how Eliot's canvas of poetic imagination presents the diverse experiences taken from the realistic society. In his poems like "Ash Wednesday" and *Four Quartets*, thought is replaced by faith. In another significant poem, "To the Indian who Died in America", Eliot points to assimilation of various cultures and identities. He says that the Indian and British soldiers who come from different backgrounds, and cultures, work for a common cause. The Indian and British soldiers, who fought the war in Africa, had come all the way from two different cultures and perspectives. Eliot's hope that the survivors of the war would come back home and narrate those experiences of suffering, anxiety and loss—whatever they had shared with those soldiers and human beings they had come across. *The Cocktail Party* is symbolically suggestive of the assimilation of varied cultures, identities and backgrounds which contribute to a new identity and living pattern. Eliot is not apprehensive of assimilating cultures, rather he addresses all those issues with a big heart. Why Eliot didn't agree to Samuel Johnson's views on metaphysical poetry that far fetched images are yoked by violence, is suggestive of the fact how heterogeneous ideas bring a more realistic and colourful picture of life. In Eliot's opinion, the intermingling of the heterogeneous ideas, thoughts and passions; seriousness and levity; intellect and emotion, do not dissociate the sensibility, rather intermingling of heterogeneous ideas and images creates organic unity in a work of art. Likewise, assimilation of various cultures, identities and perspectives in Eliot's poetry and plays makes his approach to art close to reality.

The exploration of phenomenal experiences like alienation, rootlessness and search for identity doesn't crop up in a vacuum. It is an indirect outcome of the realistic growth of society. Many critics see Eliot's poetry manifest in loneliness and alienation, which would be a partial and incomplete projection of Eliot, the poet. Therefore, it will be in the fitness of things to explore the phenomenal experiences like alienation, rootlessness and spiritual sterility—all of which are a by-product of the endless growth of the realistic society. The Wellesque utopia of scientific romance ironically turns into alienation, rootlessness and dilemma. Unlike I.A. Richards, Eliot is averse to exploration of every shade, color, design and opening up of multifoliate layers of meanings. In "Semantic Theory", Richards goes on to explore various layers of meaning as a classroom reading. Eliot, on the other hand, is a hard taskmaster. He can't afford to be irresolute in his exposition of the modern wasteland. Eliot, unlike Richards, allows his realistic exposition of "a heap of broken images" to aesthetically ratiocinate in his private workshop of poetry. Eliot instead aesthetically scans all the discursive experiences which constitute his vastness of imagination.

Thomas Stearns Eliot was born in USA and educated at Harvard. He met Ezra Pound in 1914, another American who shaped him up, turning him into a poet-critic. It was Ezra Pound who brought Eliot to literary limelight. It was Pound who primarily persuaded and inspired Eliot to get settled in England. In 1927, Eliot underwent a change of heart and acquired British citizenship. He was later anglicized by the Church of England. As a consequence, Eliot carried with him the currents and cross-currents of American sensibility while living in Boston. As Eliot was a realist, it was rather difficult for him to skip and escape all those experiences of alienation which he had come across in Boston. What is fascinating is that Eliot applied a different intonation and poetic style in order to explore the phenomenal experiences like alienation, spiritual sterility and isolation assumed a satiric expression. He invented a new tone and tenor and individual poetic style—a more realistic approach to poetry. It was Ezra Pound who cast poetry in the mould of prose. For him poetry should be as simple as a good piece of prose. Ezra Pound also redrafted Eliot's "The Wasteland", clipped and curtailed, turning it into a work of art. As such, diverse identities, cultures, perspectives and backgrounds fall into the hearth of his private workshop of poetry giving rise to a new identity, a new set of behavior, a new tone and tenor to man living in the postmodern world.

The present book will prove useful for students and teachers of English literature, particularly for those who have proclivity to understand subtle nuances of modern poetry and new criticism. It will also be useful for researches intending to work in these areas.

Adibur Rahman

Contents

	Preface	*v*
1.	Introduction	1
2.	T.S. Eliot: A Revaluation	6
3.	Eliot, Yeats and Ezra Pound	17
4.	Assimilation of Identities	34
5.	Eliot and Function of the New Critics	58
6.	A Cross-cultural Perspective	74
7.	Post Script	103
	Bibliography	120
	Index	125

1

Introduction

T.S. Eliot's place in modern poetry is something different from that of his contemporaries. He belongs to both the American and the British traditions. But Eliot was more of the American than of the British tradition. He feels the throbbing pulse of the homelessness of the American people, which in turn made him realistically see the decline of the tradition the Americans had gone through. The Americans felt cut off and isolated from the mainstream society. Robert Frost laments at the growing cult of urbanization which devastated the naturalness and simplicity of the rural landscapes. The Americans revelled in experimenting new form, meters, rhythms and all those rhetorical devices that made their poetry different from what the British did. What is striking is that Eliot does not wholly belong either to the American or to the British tradition. What needs to be realistically argued is that Eliot by his allusions, symbols and rhetorical devices manages to evoke the two voices; 'You and I' that intrinsically go on to remain inherent in the self. 'You and I' are thus the two aspects of the same coin. The basic driving force behind Eliot's projection of the objective co-relative lies in his yearning desire for concealing and restraining those manifold and discursive voices. The objective co-relative thus employed by Eliot enables him to echo the manifold voices of the self. What can basically be argued is that the perception implicit in the personal and subjective experiences goes on to persist as the basic-infrastructure of the objective co-relative. What is striking is that if personal experiences emerge as the primary perception of the artist; the objective co-relative emerges as an extended metaphor of the erstwhile personal and subjective emotions. Eliot is basically a realist; the feelings and the immediate experiences Eliot intermingles in his private workshop of poetry, are thus an indirect outcome of those subjective feelings that exist at the grass-root level. It is in this sense Eliot owes much to F.H. Bradley for his emphasis on self-fulfilment. F.H. Bradley is of the view that a work of art cannot achieve transcendence unless he concentrates on the inertia of the self. As Eliot was deeply rooted in the American tradition, the rhetorical devices, symbols and images and above all the language of the metropolis he employs, evinces at length the homelessness of the American people. Thus, Eliot intends to restrain and cover up those elements of anguish that he had himself experienced while writing his early poetry. Eliot is inescapably aware of the discordant voices that embroil him in great dissipation, melancholy and despair. Eliot is a poet of the metropolis. He looks at the realistic and illusive society that emerges in the real world making man bewilder at the crossroads. What is ironical is that the conflict that is seen taking place between the self and the real world constitutes the inbuilt processes of splitting up the self not from within but also from without. Each and every character portrayed in Eliot's poetry is a by-product of the realistic society. Eliot's protagonist hardly hears the voice of the self; he does not look back with a sense of anger rather he ends up getting embroiled in the ethnological confusion. Eliot holds that the whole humanistic movement geared up for upkeep and welfare of the mankind which 'ends not with a bang but a whimper'.[1]

Keeping in view of the above, it can however be said that 'ripeness is all' for Eliot's protagonist. Thus, the logic behind the objective co-relative carved out by Eliot, is basically a way out to address the anguish and dilemma emanating from the discordant and diverse perspectives man passes though in the postmodern society. Eliot makes use of the varied references to Dante, Baudlair and Laforgue which make poetry more complex and multidimensional. The images, symbols and the rhetorical devices employed by Eliot cannot be explained and analyzed unless the objective co-relative or the series of images are taken to be an intermediary or a medium or a vehicle of striking a balance between the immediate experience and dissociation of sensibility. What Eliot critically endeavors is to seek diverse ways and means to evolve a mechanism or an art of ambivalence with a view to accommodating varied perspectives and identities in a work of art.

Eliot's poetry is thus an extended metaphor of the realistic cult of poetry. He poetically manages to apply an all out effort to make his poetry a reflection of whatever he saw taking place in the 'real' world. Eliot and Flaubert stand at different poles. In other words, they are two poles set apart against each other. Flaubert on the other hand was well-aware of the aesthetic emotion which mysteriously gets evocative in the externalities of the 'real' world. Vyvor Winters taking note of Eliot's realistic account of poetry, regards him merely as a poet of 'automation'. Eliot's poetry, says Vyvor, is devoid of the aesthetic emotion. The new critics were well-aware of the 'fill up the gapes' that need to be looked into and examined thoroughly. Eliot undeniably made a revolution by setting a new tone and tenor in the contemporary criticism. His declaration that his true identity lay in the classical tradition, set a new tradition in poetry. "Poetry", says he, "is not a turning loose of emotion; it is an escape from emotion. Poetry is not the escape of emotion, it is an escape from emotion"; gave a new twist and turn to the concept of analyzing a work of art. His theory of impersonality is that the more is the degree of impersonality a writer practises, the larger would be the degree of perfection in his art—gave a new space to the new critics.

Similarly "honest criticism and sensitive appreciation is directed not upon the poet but upon the poetry".[2] But such function of poetry was not enough for the new critics to follow the stance Eliot had taken. A new crop of new critics hence became a new trend setter of 'elucidation and correction of taste'. It can however be said that T.S. Eliot can also be regarded as a new critic paving a way for a new turf of New Criticism.

Eliot was the creation of Ezra Pound. What Pound had earnestly aspired for was to ideographically create poetry. Poetry for Pound would be no different from the pictures as seen in ideographs. Eliot might have drawn inspiration of creating objectivity in a work of art. Matthew Arnold on the one hand enthusiastically wanted to create 'disinterestedness' in a work of art; Ezra Pound categorically was keen on creating poetry the way ideographs emerge in a work of art. F.R. Leavis gives a new definition of morality. To identify the processes how the existing order moves and to see which elements of tradition was relevant to the present generation, to F.R. Leavis—was the real basis on which he made a distinction between moral and immoral; relevant and irrelevant. It was Pound's emphasis on making poetry akin to ideographs that enabled him to give a new look to Eliot's *The Wasteland*. Eliot wrote a new kind of poetry which moves round the significance of preserving cultural standards. His poetry takes us from the real to the cross cultural world.

Eliot was bewildered at the pace with which the decline of the cultural standards inundated the socio-cultural fabric of the indigenous society. He came to find the contemporary society fragile and vulnerable to the intra-cultural world. The exposition of the realistic society he makes presents a bleak scenario in which varied cultures with their diverse propositions, preferences and inclinations, get interacted with one another, giving rise to a new, cultural, racial and religious identity. The phenomenal experiences like clash culture and culture-shock make a direct impact upon the behavioral patterns of people of diverse cultures, identities and perspectives. The growth of the emergence of the global culture in the present socio-economic scenario needs to be built with more care, insight and attention. The endless growth of the commercialized industrial society further caused cleavage and isolation amidst people living in the cross-cultural world. With the rapid growth of urbanization, people of diverse cultures and perspectives have no choice but to get migrated to the metropolis. Therefore, it is imperative on the part of him, says Eliot, to apply the corrective measure to restrain the decline of the cultural and ethnological confusion; Matthew Arnold regards such deviation from the mainstream culture as 'anarchy', which to him cuts deep into the fabric of the socio-cultural society. V.S. Naipaul in his various writings and novels while living in the new alien surroundings found himself undergo a tormenting and suffocating experience. Naipaul probes the impact of cross-cultural outlook upon the society itself and shows how man in the post-modern setup remains caught up in his behavioral patterns irrespective of the root, culture and the anchorage he belongs to. What Eliot wants is to undo the harm caused by the cultural and ethnological confusion in every sphere of life; sex, marriage and fulfilment.

A cross-cultural perspective opens up new horizons of looking up into the new living system. Man while living in the cross-cultural scenario has no way out but to receive the jerks and jolts generated by the cross-cultural identity. It is in this sense that Eliot's declaring himself as a classicist holds much water. In Eliot's exposition of the realistic cross-cultural society, the need of spiritual anchorage becomes more poignant and sharp after Eliot crossed over to the British Isles. The present appreciation of Eliot's poetry brings into focus the clash of the two traditions; the British and American. What is striking is that Eliot's poetry, his plays and his other critical writings, point out at how Eliot looks at the contemporary society from a Britisher's eye. The Laforguian impact, hence can be seen in Eliot's employing the symbols, images and metaphors which, in clear-cut way, communicates to the man living in the metropolis. In such a scenario where cultural aberration and ethnological confusion prevail in the fabric of the socio-cultural society, assertion of identity to him is the last resort through which the cultural sanctity can be restored to the post-modern society. Richard Wright, Chinua Achebe even Joseph Conrad and Graham Greene also realistically look at the new avalanche of the cross-cultural behavior.

NOTES

1. T.S. Eliot, *The Hollow Men, Selected Poems*, Faber and Faber, ed. 1980, p. 80.
2. T.S. Eliot, *Tradition and The Individual Talent*, p. 20.

2

T.S. Eliot: A Revaluation

Assimilation of identities is one of the peculiar characteristics that make his poetry distinct from his contemporaries. In Eliot's canvas of poetry, verisimilitude and intermingling of identities can realistically be seen in all its tapestry. Eliot was bewildered at the pace of assimilation of identities which phantasmagorically haunted at the back of his mind. What was bewildering to Eliot was the pace with which the assimilation of ideas, backgrounds, cultures and identities broke and amalgamated into one single identity. In Nehruvian's concept of composite culture, each and every integral of the composite culture is tied up to each other in a harmonious chord. Every integral of his composite culture essentially has its own color and identity, but at the same time it naturally falls into the mainstream of the composite society. In Eliot's concept of civilization, identities—racial, cultural, and ethnic and socio-political—existing in the milieu have been depicted with a great variety.

Day Lewis' *The Magnetic Mountain* (1933) tended to search for a new track for political and economic structure. W.H. Auden who had proclivity to the left orthodoxy had argued for a new interpretation of art. He was of the view that Marx-Freud marriage would create new inroads into the human psyche. Christopher Caudwell's dictum that poetry is a criticism of society, in identical ways opened up new floodgates of the socialistic interpretation of art. Art, says Christopher Caudwell, is a by-product of society. For Caudwell understanding of finer sensibilities of art is something akin to understanding society and the problems emanating from. In his opinion, every form of art is based upon the emancipation of society. It is in this context that he differentiates illusion from reality. Caudwell basically opines that art too can create emancipation on the social plane—is the basic assumption that makes him realize how art is a powerful instrument of identifying assimilation of varied cultures, milieu, races and perspectives. Eliot who was all praise for classical scholars, was at the same time became the founder of new school of criticism. In his various essays and writings, Eliot writes that honest criticism is made not on the poet but upon poetry. The new critics like I.A. Richards, F.R. Leavis, William Empson and Cleanth Brooks felt the need to interpret and analyze nuances of art and literature putting more emphasis on the verbal criticism. Eliot on the one hand was a staunch classicist. He was pre-occupied with the idea of streamlining the tradition with the existing order. In the same vein, Eliot's bafflement persists somewhere in the areas lying in between the poet and his poetry. The critics beginning their literary criticism right from the area, say the new critics lies between the poet and his poetry. The new critics pay no less emphasis on the irony, tension and motley colours of meaning and interpretation that emanated from the text itself. In other words, new criticism sought to establish a balance between absurdity and brilliance. William Empson explains the possibilities of seven types of ambiguities concentrating on symbols, images and allusions emerging into the mind of the reader. New criticism tends to seek the most obscure and difficult meaning out of meaning. It thus makes new criticism more complex. New criticism is thus a new kind of criticism which is devoid of the pre-emption that Eliot draws up in his concept of criticism. New criticism thus brings into focus the impact of psycho analytical criticism according to which inner cleavage of the human mind too plays a crucial role in the analysis of a work of art. Freud and Jung contributed to taking the cult of criticism to a new scale of heights. Odgen and I.A. Richards explore new shades and contours of meaning to semantics and evocative theory of poetry. Richards in his principle of criticism and practical criticism basically puts emphasis on devising other ways and means to find new horizons that could widen and pitch fork a better understanding of the text. As a result the new critics unlike Eliot weren't pre-empted with analyzing poetry with all the objective co-relatives that make poetry impersonal. He was preoccupied with the ethos that in Eliot's opinion enriches art and literature at every existing order. Though F.R. Leavis was a disciple of Eliot, yet he gives a new turn and twist to the cotemporary tenets of criticism which was very much influenced by the literary scenes built up by Eliot and his followers. As Eliot's poetry is a creation of Ezra pound, F.R. Leavis too finds his roots somewhere in Eliot's elaboration of criticism. Frontiers of criticism, says F.R. Leavis, can't be kept barricaded and limited to the sense of history and the sense of tradition. From F.R. Leavis' standpoint, the true relevance of criticism remains inherent in drawing up and defining the 'producible text'. Both Ezra Pound and T.S. Eliot show distrust of democratic tendencies in politics. Many a contemporary milieu was a product of the social problems emanating from maintaining the cultural standards. In 1932, a new cult of imitating Eliot arose on the literary horizon. Political and economic forces at work demanded new poets to emerge on the literary horizon and tackle the problems emanating from Eliot's pre-emptive bid of maintaining cultural standards—is indicative of the basic fact how Eliot's bafflement knew no bounds at man's being culturally defunct from the mainstream society as the fear existing on the psychic plane at man's aberration from the cultural standards. Criticism, says F.R. Leavis, should be made intelligible to intellectuals in general interpretation of tradition and historicity. Weston in her book, *From Ritual to Romance* applies a mythological study of the symbols and images applied by Eliot. F.R. Leavis, on the other hand, in his numerous essays of criticism, makes morality an integral part of the frontiers of criticism. Leavis castigates Eliot for the obscurity that becomes a stumbling block to the reader's comprehension. Christopher Caudwell unlike Eliot and the new critics gave new meanings and dimensions to the perception of analysis of a work of art. Christopher's tenets of criticism are based on social criticism in which a work of art is put to the spur of criticism from the sociological perspective. With the emergence of the new sociological world-order, a work of art says Caudwell, needs to be analyzed and seen from the sociological perspective. It wouldn't be out of place to bring into focus the poets like W.H. Auden and Stephen Spender who sociologically argued for making a new solidarity by their proclivity to the left orthodoxy. Caudwell's canons of social criticism unlike Eliot's neither takes into account the sense of history nor the ambiguities that promoted Empson to explore the most difficult meaning out of meaning to art and creativity. Caudwell instead resorted to a new kind of social criticism in which social strata give new innuendos and insinuations of meanings. In his remarkable essay, "Poetry and Science", I.A. Richards plays the role of a new critic. Playing the role of a new critic, Richards puts emphasis on knowing new form of experience. He is artistically concerned with seeing each every cadence of poetry which makes effect after effect upon the inner mind of the reader. Leavis takes into account all the paraphernalia which Eliot pronounces at length in his various theories of criticism. Leavis clarifies that mere analysis and interpretation; parallelism and contrast are not the real function of true criticism. Disagreeing with Eliot what Leavis opines is that the basic function of a critic is to confine his self to the 'producible text'. Leavis explains and defines areas in which he finds obligatory on the part of him to draw up a line of demarcation between scrutiny and New Criticism. The new critics hold the belief that the real function of criticism lies inherent in the exercise of verbal and structural mechanism that accelerates various shades, contours and meanings to the extent of the most difficult and ultimate meaning.

New Criticism basically originates from a verbal complex of tensions, ironies and paradoxes emanating from poetry. The new critics are of the view that nuances of new criticism are far more practicable than analyzing poetry from the biographical and sociological perspectives. It takes into account all those subtleties of ironies and verbal connotations that exist from within. Analyzing poetry beyond the intentions with which a particular work of art, nonetheless is the basic driving force that gives impetus to gather new space for new criticism. The new critics were hell bent upon defining and discerning the distance and the gap that lay between the poet and his poetry. They cannot afford to live into the illusive area: existing in between the poet and his poetry. New Criticism does not keep itself at par with the social and historical backgrounds while interpreting a work of art. The new critics on the other hand believe that ignoring various shades of the verbal and structural connotations emanating from poetry—is something tantamount to restraining and dismantling the original interpretation of a work of art. Eliot, Wimsatt, Empson and F.R. Leavis were however conscious of the limitations of the archetypal, social and above all of the Marxist interpretations of a work of art. It was this perspective to which the new critics rose to the literary horizon. They found themselves utterly disillusioned with the concept of historical perspective of criticism. It was basically a reactionary movement for showing contempt not only for historical criticism but also for social interpretation of a work of art. The origin of the school of New Criticism takes place in the first book of Robert Graves and William Empson. During the thirties, there had been an incessant search for bringing out the most difficult meaning out of a work of art. In order to give vent to the principles of New Criticism both the verbal and structural analyses which were practised during the 1930s thus became the basis on which the foundation of New Criticism was practically to take place. The two articles entitled as "The International Fallacy" and "The Affective Fallacy", which were respectively written by W.K. Wimsatt Jr. and Monroe C. Bradley poignantly argued that the two of the assumption indoctrinated in romantic criticism were taken to be fallacious. The basic assumption implicit in the nuances of New Criticism discern to "The design or intention of the author is neither available nor desirable as a standard of judging the success of a work of literary art;"[1] this is how Wimsatt and Beardsley protest in their articles. The doctrine of New Criticism is thus made up of two parts. Firstly, the design or intention of the author categorically cannot be ascertained from the biological and historical perspectives. Nuances of New Criticism in the sense of their deliberation intend to derive the standard of criticism from the psychological perspective. The function of the new critic is not to find new emotions to analyze various shades of meaning and experiences taking place on the psychic and intellectual planes. The purpose of new critics intends to bring into focus new form of meanings, undertones and ambiguities operating on the verbal and structural planes irrespective of those original intentions which might have moved up and inspired the mind of the artist at the time of its inception and creativity. It can thus however be said that the doctrine of New Criticism was an eye-opener for those critics who single-handedly relied on the biographical and historical methods of interpretation. Allen Tate and Cleanth Brooks were the later disciples of Robert Graves-Wimsatt school of criticism that opened up a new horizon for poetry to treat poetry for the sake of poetry. The new shades of meaning promoted by T.S. Eliot, I.A. Richards, William Empson and F.R. Leavis thus created new areas of criticism taking them up to the sixties. Eliot and Wimsatt while setting up their tones argued for differentiating literature from biography. F.R. Leavis on the other hand argued for drawing up a new line of demarcation between philosophy and sociology. Wimsatt, on the other hand, argued for distinguishing the verbal connotations of the text from the psychological constraints taking place on the psychic plane. It can thus etymologically be argued that Eliot, Wimsatt and Empson created new areas of interest in the field of literary criticism. It was John Crowe Ramson's book *The New Criticism* (1941) in which the term was for the first time propounded. Wimsatt in his collection "The Verbal Icon" (1954) evinces the varied, subtle complex meaning and ambiguities emanating from a work of art which may not be in congruity with all those intentions which the author might have kept in mind at the time of its creativity. Hence, the new factors leading to the inbuilt psychic processes and ambiguities thereof, create a new critical awareness; a new twist and turn to his faculty of appreciating a work of art irrespective of the historical and mythical methods applied by his school of criticism. The new critics however cannot afford to rely on the sociological and historical interpretation. Instead having shifted their area of criticism from historical interpretation of art to the verbal and structural vehicle of criticism, they practically opened up new horizons for a better understanding of art and literature in which varied iota and shapes of meaning are put on to the miniature. Dylan Thomas recognized much earlier the danger of building rich structures of rhythms and without allowance for necessary pipes and plumbing of reasonable meaning. He felt the need to innovate a new type of structure. The social poets of the thirties, Auden and Spender employed rhetoric and images taken from the sociological aspect. For them poetry was something 'reporting' in favor of poetry as individual development or self-unravelling under the impact of Marx and Freud. Dylan Thomas unlike Spender and Auden is said to have been made under the spell of Old Testament and Freud. The new apocalypse disliked anachronism.

Eliot while analyzing the works of Baudlair holds the belief that the modern poets should put emphasis on employing images and symbols in order to project the multi-dimensional aspects of the metropolis. To Eliot, London is an unreal city; the symbols like cactus, stone and fog realistically point out at the splitting and crumbling process of the modern wasteland. In "The Use of Poetry and Use of Criticism", Eliot says that a poet's existence lay 'some where between the poet and that reader'. He is of the view that the larger is the degree of refinement in culture, the larger would be poetic sensibility, taste, perception and refinement. Eliot eloquently writes, "The poetry of a people takes its life from the people's speech and in turn gives life to it; and represents its highest point of consciousness, its greatest power and its most delicate sensibility."[2]

Eliot's theory of criticism emphasizes discarding emotion infusing a sense of history and a sense of tradition into the texture of his creative art in which the ethos and his milieu essentially remain manifest—is one of the hallmarks of his tenets of criticism. What is significant is that Eliot limits his art to the mere analysis and critical interpretation of various nuances of art. Eliot's elaboration of his theory of criticism is thus necessarily limited to his emphasis on impersonality and objective presentation of art. F.R. Leavis on the other hand unlike Eliot explains the modus operandi of his critical faculty to emphasize the need to present only those nuances of art which are relevant to the producible text. In "Tradition and the Individual Talent", Eliot talks of the basic fact that poetry is not the turning loose of emotion but an escape from emotion; it is not the expression of personality but an escape from personality. The new critics, in such a scenario found themselves in a state of bafflement as Eliot evinces the function of the critics in between the poet and his poetry. Honest criticism, Eliot writes, is made not upon the poet but upon poetry. As such the critics during the 1920s gathered round and emphasized the need to gear up a more dynamic role of criticism in which the play of verbal and structural criticism was given a more dynamic role to find new possible avenues of interpretation of a work of art for seeking honest interpretation of a work of art. Leavis goes one step ahead of Eliot. Being conscious of the limitations of Eliot's canons of criticism, he argues for intermingling only those elements of the past which are relevant to the existing order. It is in this sense F.R. Leavis places the meaning of the producible text. I.A. Richards who is critical of Eliot's elaboration of critical theories, in his theory of criticism points out how Eliot ignores the play of impulse which too plays an important role in the evocativeness of the self. Freud, on the one hand, psycho-analytically says that each and every addition of internal monologues stirs up the sum total of the ideas which remain hidden in the receptacle of the human psyche transforming the inner being of man. Eliot is averse to the impulse, 'the inner voice' and to all those subjective co-relatives that become manifest in a work of art at its very inception and creativity. Man with a new addition of the ideas flowing into the human psyche undergoes a sea-change; the power of ratiocination makes a great impact upon the inner cleavage of the receptacle of the human mind. I.A. Richards, too like Freud, made the aesthetic sense the basis of his principles of criticism. Likewise, Richards while elaborating his canons of criticism says that the human psyche is brought into a state of commotion after receiving fresh impetus from the impulse enabling itself to yield to that system of impulses which brings satisfaction to the being of man. Richards, in his various critical writings thus establishes a new relation between the mind and the impulse. For him a balance established between the substance of the human mind and the inbuilt impulse, says Richards, should be made the fulcrum of analyzing a work of art ignoring which the aesthetic sense cannot be brought into play. Hence, it can logically be argued that function of a critic lies confined not into the jargons of the objective co-relatives. What makes a work of art life-like, says Richards, is a perfect harmony of every play of the impulse adding up a new identity. Eliot makes tradition and individual talent coexist with each other whereas the new critics vehemently argue that the role and function of a critic cannot be kept confined to mere analysis, contrast and parallelism and to the objective co-relatives for a wider and comprehensive interpretation of art. The new critics, thus probe how the conflict, ambiguity and paradox take place within a work of art. A wider horizon and practicability could be created in order to make interpretation of a work of art go a full circle. Herbert Read, says Eliot, was hell bent upon the biographical criticism explicitly taking into account the incidents and the backgrounds which might have shaped up his childhood or the books he might have read or the persons who he might have come across before creating a work of art. New Criticism on the other hand emerged on the literary scene of the 1920s and 1930s to play a more dynamic role that could give varied shades of meaning irrespective of the socialistic, historical and biographical methods. They could not either afford to limit criticism to the cloister of the biographical or historical method of criticism, instead to them, multiple shades of meaning; dilemma, ambiguities, paradox and irony emanating from a work of art—are more important than making criticism a slave to the historical and biographical methods of criticism.

As Eliot was deeply rooted in the American tradition, the backgrounds and the influences which shaped him up always remained at the back of his mind. The technique of objective co-relative which he carves out, figures at length how dissociation of sensibility takes place making it part of the larger consciousness. The basic problem before Eliot thus was how to conceal emotions corroding him from within. Perhaps Eliot's bafflement lay somewhere in the subjective co-relatives that always menacingly remained at the back of his mind. The objective co-relative he employs in his poetry, enables him to conceal non-art-emotion. The purpose of turning his non-art-emotion, says Eliot, into art-emotion is to restrain the subjective co-relative which is part and parcel of the larger consciousness. Eliot's theory of criticism and his elaboration of objective co-relative do not exist in the vacuum instead the varied elements of subjectivity which play a significant role in the making of Eliot, act as a parapet to conceal those subjective emotions which remain deep-seated into the inner recesses of his mind. The symbols yoked within the framework of his objective co-relatives—is a conscious effort not to allow the multitude of emotion to get infused into the work of art. In Eliot's poem "Love Song of J. Alfred Prufrock", the protagonist undergoes a state of dilemma before unfolding his mind. The basic reason behind his inability to make resolution is the emergence of the diverse ideas flowing into the flux of his mind. He feels himself pass through a Hamlet-like-situation finding himself unable to make the proposal. The varied thoughts emerging into his mind make him caught up in irresolution and dilemma. In "Portrait of a Lady" the protagonist receives tremors of shock at the way the elderly lady makes her proposal of love. Eliot thus employs a series of images and symbols to bring into focus the canvas of the inner psyche and the dilemma which take possession of the self of the protagonist. Eliot's place in modern poetry is thus something different from that of his contemporaries. Unlike Auden and Spender Eliot belongs to both the American and the British traditions. Taking into account the pros and cons of his later poetry, it can be logically argued that Eliot was more of the American tradition than of the British tradition. Eliot realistically could see the splitting up of the American tradition and its consequences thereof. He saw the homelessness of the American people which in turn made him conceal the influx of the subjective co-relatives which evocate remaining surged within. Eliot was well aware of the power that remained inlay and superimposed within the self. It was rather difficult for Eliot to conceal those subjective co-relatives which always kept alive the belonging of the self. As such Eliot was in need of concealing his bafflement by virtue of employing the usage of the objective co-relative. Eliot never looks back with anger instead he looks back with all his despair and melancholy that envelope all his being. Thus, the diverse assimilation of identities and perspectives multiply the grief and melancholy made inroads into his psyche transforming him into a new identity. The dramatic personae Eliot portrays can be seen grappling with assimilation of identities. His play, *The Cocktail Party*, is hence, symbolically suggestive of assimilation of diverse identities taking place in the illusive realistic society. Unlike Yeats, Eliot does not go nostalgic; he rather prefers to address all those problems emanating from assimilation of identities. As such he follows up and adopts the technique formulated by Laforgue to accommodate those discursive experience emerging at length at various stages of his life. Finding himself in the alien surroundings he hardly knows how to co-relate tradition with the individual talent. The Americans felt independent, cut-off and drifted from the mainstream of the British tradition. They revelled in experimenting new forms, meters and rhythms in their usage of the poetic and colloquial rhetoric. What is striking is that Eliot does not wholly belong to either of the two traditions—the American and the British tradition. Eliot by employing his allusions, symbols and rhetorical devices manages to conceal and cover up all those subjective emotions which make him a great critic.

NOTES

1. George Watson, *The Literary Critics*, Penguin Books, ed. 1964, p. 222.
2. T.S. Eliot, *The Use of Poetry and Use of Criticism*, Faber and Faber, London, p. 15.

3

Eliot, Yeats and Ezra Pound

Eliot's poetry is the poetry of bafflement; the bafflement which evokes assimilation of the varied perspectives, voices, milieu and identities. E.M. Forster like Eliot was tormented by the problem of clash culture. Forster addresses the problem of culture in identical ways. Man in the Forsterian world can be seen grappling with the problem of clash culture and its after effects emanating from it. What Forster is basically concerned at showing them prevailing in the post-modern society which was totally alien to them. But Forster had tenacity to make a common passage though which people of varied races, backgrounds, cultures and milieu could live in harmony. Eliot and V.S. Naipaul too have proclivity to addressing the problem of identity in the alien surroundings. Naipaul looks back not with anger but with a sense of nostalgia to see his roots with a renewed vision. Attainment of knowledge in Eliot's domain of poetry has negative bearings to his quest of freedom. The real world, which Eliot perceives, lies not in the colossal growth of knowledge rather in the redemptive measures taken up by self-realization forms the basic source of reasoning of his stance of life.

Eliot's poems are an incessant search for inventing a vocabulary; a rhetorical device, which could accommodate multitude of identities. Yeats puts emphasis on the multitude of emotions whereas, in Eliot's poetry, the process of dismantling and splitting up of personality start taking place with emergence of the scientific and humanistic progresses. Spiritual sterility hence is an outcome of the endless scientific and industrial developments. It was D.H. Lawrence who with all his sincerity and tenderness evoked his dissent with the colossal growth of science. In "Rainbow" and "Women in Love", Lawrence, optimistically agitates the cult of worshipping the scientific facts. On the other hand, man in Eliot's world, does not look back with anger, he looks back with a sense of melancholy and despair. Eliot realized the pathetic fallacy hidden in the colossal growth of science and intellect, which to him, no longer caters to aesthetic emotion. What is ironical is that a pattern of gloom, pessimism and melancholy envelops the whole being of Eliot; the poet who could envision how diverse perspectives and identities torment man on the psychic and intellectual planes. It can thus be said that characters which Eliot depicts in his modern poetry, are sad and pessimistic groping in the dark finding no hope in their attainment of 'knowledge' and all sorts of scientific and economic developments they have achieved, says Eliot, cannot achieve transcendence. Eliot writes, "after such knowledge what forgiveness?" ironically points out that they are a spiritually lost generation having no sense of belonging. As in Eliot's poetry, man feels himself caught up in dilemma-like situation; characters portrayed on the canvas of his poetry, are spiritually lackluster; they are haunted by their own irresolution. Being beset with the diverse cultures, perspectives and backgrounds, man in Eliot's domain of poetry feels the evocativeness of his self. The pallor of gloom and despair goes on to cut deep into him as he finds himself spiritually dislocated from the mainstream socio-cultural order. What is bewildering to Eliot is that he does not know how to tackle the problem emanating from amalgamation of diverse identities, cultures and perspectives. George Orwell in *Animal Farm* identically grapples with the problems of mingling identities. Man in the Orwellian world, has been shown embarrassed at the concealment of identities. It is the vehicle of double-speak, which enables him to camouflage his stark emotion. Yeats is bewildered at the arrival of the beastly and violent generation. Eliot on the other hand was bewildered at tackling the problem of assimilating identities in the post-modern world. For Eliot getting stream-lined with the tradition and the sense of history could alone create a sense of belonging. Nothing less than identity, says Eliot, would give comfort to man. What is ironical is that Eliot never looks into the root cause of the spiritual degeneration which he regards as a by-product of the realistic growth of society. He keeps his eyes wide open on the ever-widening consciousness, the consciousness taking place on the scientific, economic cultural planes in the illusive 'real' world, which he thinks hardly creates the third dimension for putting up his stance of life on the aesthetic plane. The real world ironically for Eliot is the ultimate truth noticed in the external world, is indifferent to the doctrine of the self.

Eliot emerged as an iconoclast disemboweling the romanticists at the periphery. He was the pioneer of resurgence of classicism back in the modern age. Being averse to emotion that essentially makes a work of art subjective, he argues for objective poetry in which emotion implicit in the artist has no role to play. In his numerous critical essays he defines poetry from a different angle, which was new to his contemporaries; "Poetry", says Eliot, "is not the turning loose of emotion, but an escape from emotion; it is not the expression of personality but an escape from personality". Defining a system how interpretation of a work of art should be done, Eliot evolves his poetic formulation saying that poetry is made not on the poet but upon poetry gives enough space to the new critics which clearly shows how Eliot was pre-empted with the concealment of emotion. His projection of the technique of objective co-relative was a vehicle to restrain the emotions implicit in him. What is striking is that Eliot was rather baffled at the way the subjective emotion implicit in him aesthetically worked within seeking definition in every work of art. As such dealing with evocativeness of emotion, for Eliot was a baffling experience. Hence, in order to seek distraction from subjective art, Eliot had to argue for interpreting art and literature in terms of time and space within the framework of religion, myth, history and tradition. For him historical fact or a sense of tradition is an unavoidable necessity. Eliot and his school of poetry gave lots of space to be filled up by the nuances of new criticism. The function of a new critic, says Eliot, is not to find new emotion rather to see whether it is in harmony with the past-ness of the past. New criticism, on the other hand, argues for interpreting a work of art irrespective of the heritage. It emphasizes interpretation of a work of art to its fullest possible extent. William Empson points out at ambiguities, which is suggestive of a variety of meanings. For him the most difficult meaning can deliver the ultimate meaning emanating from a work or art. Keeping in view of the nuances of new criticism, the new critics like I.A. Richards, William Empson, F.R. Leavis and even Virginia Woolf had their own canons of interpreting a work of art. I.A. Richards in his principles of criticism gives priority to the subjective emotions, which play a crucial role in the process of creativity. Richards who was himself a disciple of Eliot, gets shifted from Eliot's stance of new space and his emphasis on linking up of the past with the present at every existing order, was aesthetically conscious of the emotions which played upon the impulses stirring them up to their satiety. William Empson, on the one hand, relentlessly argues for bringing out the most difficult meaning out of meaning. Empson, unlike Eliot, emphasizes currents and cross-currents of the interpretations of a work of art that go on to flow into the inner psyche. The inner conflict causing tension into the interiors of the human mind, says Empson, evokes the most difficult meaning. Empson carries out all those ideas, thought patterns and images, which emerge on to the smoke screen of the human mind. The new critics thus unlike Eliot and his followers, were pre-occupied with their intention of taking into account all those images and ideas whatsoever come into the emerging consciousness of the human mind. Thus, New Criticism aims at the most difficult meaning. The origin of New Criticism was thus defined in the first work of Robert Graves and William Empson before the verbal and structural analysis was in vogue even before 1930. As Eliot emphasized the sense of history, and historical manifestoes in the United States, became in vogue during the 1930s and 1940s. However, it can be said that the literary studies framed up by Eliot, Richards, Empson and F.R. Leavis paved the way for New Criticism which had dominance on the literary horizon up to 1960. The critical theories propounded by Eliot, Wimsatt and

Empson were regarded as a movement emerging in the form of New Criticism. The business of the new critics thus lives confined to discarding the historical, archetypal and biographical methods to go for the most difficult meaning says Graves is the ultimate object of good reading. Somerset Maugham in his "Summing Up" regards pleasure as the principal driving force of good and enjoyable reading. Maugham critically says that it is the element of pleasure, which basically makes reading enjoyable. Taking into account the limitation of Eliot's concept of criticism, the new critics were harsh on historical criticism. As such, New Criticism during the 1940s became fashionable. Cleanth Brooks and Robert Penn Warren in their anthology, *Understanding Poetry*, assailed in its preface saying that "if poetry is worth-teaching at all, it is worth-teaching on poetry".

Being a new critic, Richards puts emphasis on the word-power emphasizing that the positive power of word inherent from within, becomes the basis of his principles. In his *Principles of Literary Criticism*, Richards elaborates the emotive function of poetry whereas in Meaning of meaning, he keeps giving shape to the evocativeness of the symbols employed in the fabric of poetry. In his *Principles of Criticism*, he concentrates on pronouncing the systematic principles of the subtle and elaborate scrutiny of verbal complexities. In his elaboration of the semantic principle, he draws up inspiration from Coleridge's view in which he regards imagination as synthetic and magical. Richards' semantic principle thus lies basically embedded to the meaning of words. William Empson on the other hand applies his critical insight in untying the knots of multiplicity of diverse meanings. The vehicle of syllogism has been dealt with taking into account the negative bearing on the problem of evolution. In *Seven Types of Ambiguities*, he basically builds up the concept of ambiguity saying that ambiguity is valuable while unfolding various types of complexities and meanings. Richards on the other hand while dealing with the meaning of meaning relies on the inherent and the aesthetic meaning; whereas Empson while classifying three kinds of ambiguities, puts on the exemplar of the third type of ambiguity of which the reader is basically unaware. A reader says Empson is faced with three categories of ambiguity; one which remains 'intelligible' in the mind. In the second type of ambiguity, the labour of bringing out the meaning or squeezing the meaning of meaning, becomes the second criteria, classifies Empson. The projection of syllogism, which he emphasizes, has a negative bearing upon the problem of evaluation of the semantics. An ambiguity says Empson never remains a stumbling block to the critical faculty of the mind, instead, it provides a better critical faculty of thought for a better understanding of art and literature. The third type of ambiguity, says Richards, is one, which works if it is never discovered. Empson more often than not intends to enter into the psyche of the author experiencing the series of the interior monologues or intentions experiencing which the author might have had—forms the basis of the 'complex words'. While building up the theory of 'complex words' he shows his tilt to a cognitive experience. Empson in his elaboration of complex 'words' does not agree to Richards' notion that emotions of words in poetry, are, 'independent of the sense'. His *Philosophy of Rhetorics*, is based upon the semantic analysis. Rhythm, says Richards, has hardly anything to do with emotion. It is not the rhythm says he rather it is the sound which matters most to the reader in his understanding of poetry. T.S. Eliot, in an identical way, in his essay, "Frontiers of Criticism", says that understanding and enjoyment are not two distinct literary activities; instead they go hand in hand. Virginia Woolf on the other hand regards the human mind as a luminous halo. Man, says she, is a product of the flux of the interior monologues that flow into the receptacle of the human mind. The French symbolists are of the view that poetry cannot express emotion directly; emotions can only be evoked. Baudlair too opines that every shade and design of the symbols, images and ideas employed in a work of art, has correspondence in their respective fields. Mallarme maintains that poetry is made not of ideas but of words. Wimsatt and Cleanth Brooks write that the doctrine of the objective co-relative puts emphasis on the anti-romantic cult of art. Unlike Pound, T.E. Hulme categorically says that poetry deals with the 'intensive'. Explaining the inherent dimensions of the 'intensive', says T.E. Hulme, that intuition is a condition for exploring the 'intensive' experiments. Hence, function of poetry, says he, is not to present the mechanical rather than the organic. In his elaboration of the semantic analysis, I.A. Richards, on the other hand, shows concern for evaluation of subtle and verbal complexities. In his *Philosophy of Rhetorics* (1936) he puts aside the traditional approach of distinguishing between 'referential and emotive aspects of language'. Hence, he argues for a new vehicle of rhetorics built up upon the semantic principle pinpointing that sound plays a more important role than rhythm. Richards reiterates that a language may be employed for the sake of reference irrespective of the basic fact that either it is true or false, can be regarded as a scientific use of poetry. The same statement used for seeing the effects of emotion and attitude can be useful for the emotive use of language. Richards makes the choice of rejection the basis of his theory. Richards' choice of synaesthesia stands for an equilibrium of the play of impulse. In his *Principles of Literary Criticism*, he elaborates the mechanism of synaesthesia through which the process of selection or rejection takes place. It is the play of the impules, which gives an added dimension to the creative power of the human psyche. Play of stirring up the impulses, thus depends upon how and up to which degree they satisfy the human mind. It is the inherent attitude, says Richards, which gives momentum to relativity of an experience. Poetry on the other hand, says Pound, should possess the virtues of good prose. He shows interest in choosing ideograph as a paradigm of the poetic method, created new ground for writing communicative poetry, which could be made more intelligible to readers. Poetry, to Pound, was thus something akin to 'inspired Mathematics'. It is a "method of juxtaposing picturable elements which means for the shallow and over simplistic distractions: it allowed a skilful artist to define with subtlety and precision what he wanted to say: not this, and not that but precisely this."[1] (1) Precision and accuracy, says he, is a condition for making poetry communicative and intelligible to masses. In "Instigations", he elaborates the ideographic method saying that it is a process in which "the use of material images, to suggest immaterial relations. (2) Poetry therefore, says Pound, "it is a sort of inspired mathematics which gives us equations, not for abstract figures, triangle, spheres and the like but equations for the human emotions."[2]

Ezra Pound was a creator of T.S. Eliot. His significant works, "Homage to Sextons Propertius" (1917) and "Hugh Selwyn Mauberley" are the poems in which Pound portrays the currents and cross-currents of the British culture. Likewise, Lawrence's "Women in Love" is a satirical work on the sharp decline in spiritual and ethical values of the contemporary society. Eliot bears resemblance to Henry James in his reaching out from tradition of America to that of Europe. Eliot shows concern at the declining social, cultural and traditional values. His adherence to the cultural values needs conformity with the historical sense without which says Eliot, there can be no harmony and aesthetic beauty in the modern society. Eliot comes out of the doctrine of the self-emphasizing the need to introspect in his search of the poetic tradition. The Flaubartian impact can be seen in Eliot's emphasis that a poet's mind should remain 'inert' and 'neutral' towards his subject matter. Baudlair blends sense impressions, Mallarme says that a poet can explore the mystery through the non-conceptual properties of words particularly in music. Eliot applies the technique of Baudlair in creating symbols and images in his poetry. The images and symbols employed in *The Wasteland* are thus an outcome of the Baudlairian impact on Eliot. S.T. Coleridge, on the other hand, was a seismologist who was concerned not only with the meaning of words but also with the behavior of words. Taking into account the behavioral aspects of word-power, it can however be said that Coleridge too opened floodgates of a new system of interpreting nuances of art from the syntactical aspects exploring the possible behavior or words that could enter into the flux of the human mind; it psychologically brings about change in the substance of the human mind. With the changes taking place into the scenario of the socio-economic and scientific developments, the new critics emphasize the need to see the function of criticism from a new vision, which was quite different from the principles of criticism propounded by Eliot and his followers. Fechner took the problem of aesthetics to laboratory. Freud in his elaboration of wit explains how the applicability of wit draws upon the unconscious. In his introduction to Psycho-analysis he opened up a new system of examining and interpreting the human mind putting emphasis on psychoanalysis. It was I.A. Richards by whose contribution, impact of psychology made an indelible imprint into the receptacle of the human mind. Unlike Pound, T.E. Hulme says that poetry deals with the intensive. Exploring the dimensions of the intensive, Hulme says that intuition is a condition for exploring the 'intensive' experiences. Function of poetry, says he, is not to present the mechanical rather than the organic. In *Speculations*, which was published in 1924, he categorically says that there is no such thing figuring out dignified subject matter. Hulme hence reacts both against Arnold's high seriousness and Coleridge's distinction between fancy and imagination. Images in verse, says he, should not be taken from the stock of the discursive language. In other words, images in verse should be an outcome of the intuitive language. Hence, Hulme takes the classical view to be identical with the 'moral religious attitude'. Function of a critic on the other hand says Eliot is not to find new emotions but to interpret them keeping it in conformity with the tradition. Eliot was critical of the contemporary critics particularly of the Romantics. In his letter written to Harriet Monroe, Pound propounds his definition of poetry in 1915. "Poetry", says he, "must be as well written as prose", simplicity and meaning are the two basic elements which must be the sole prerequisite of poetry. In Pound's domain of poetry, there is no room for paraphrases and inversions. He sets aside the set phrases, rhymes that are produced for the sake of rhythm. The role of rhythm in Pound's scheme of poetry conveys and delivers meaning keeping in view of precision and simplicity. Great literature, says Pound, should always be charged with "meaning to the utmost possible degree".[3] Pound principally puts emphasis on the method of the Chinese ideographs. His ideographic method is a synchronization of concrete particulars.

It was I.A. Richards who for the first time saw the role of psychology in giving a new shape to English criticism. Elaborating his concept of criticism in his numerous works like *Principles of Criticism*, and *Coleridge on Imagination*, he says that poetry without the aid of psychology will be meaningless and incomplete. Any such attempt applied into the nature of poetry would be vain. Richards reiterates that psychology is the indispensable instrument for interpreting nuances of art and literature in the correct perspective. In the Selected Essays, Eliot argues for amalgamating diverse experiences into an organic whole. Eliot was influenced by Jules Laforgue and Tristan Corbiere. It was the impact of Pound by virtue of which he coined the objective correlative. Objective correlative to Eliot is a series of objects: a situation or chain of events, which shall be the formula of restraining that particular emotion. Pound in an identical way defines poetry as equations for human emotions. Poetry, says Eliot, is not the turning loose of emotion but escape from emotion. In order to justify his emphasis on objectivity, Eliot says that a set of images or a chain of situations help restrain subjective emotions. In order to clarify his concept of poetry he says that Shakespeare's *Hamlet* is a correlative, which restrains subjectivity. Reacting on Eliot's concept of objectivity, Ransom finds Eliot's theory of criticism as "too psychologistic and less Cognitive". Winters Vyvor like Ransom identically says that Eliot's classicism is not classical in letter and spirit. As such Eliot seems to be influenced by Pound's view that poetry is something akin to inspired mathematics. Therefore, Eliot's objective co-relative seems to have derived from Pound's co-relation of poetry with inspired mathematics. His technique of objective correlative is a set of objects: a situation of events, which shall be the formula of presenting truth with objectivity. Pound on the one hand projects possible equation for human emotions, Eliot on the other hand argues for drawing up impersonal experiences.

There is a striking difference between Eliot and poets of the thirties. For Eliot myth, religion and philosophy are more important than art. In his parameter of poetry, art is a rhetorical device for creating communication. Art is a pedestal in Eliot's poetry through which he puts emphasis on the preservation of culture by linking up the past with the existing order. To Eliot any such deviation from the milestone of tradition would be tantamount to deviating from that of anarchy. Art is a medium through which Eliot classically raises his voice in which philosophy; classicism; myth and religion lay at the upper most. G.B. Shaw considers art as subsidiary in his propaganda of his Shavian philosophy. Even the poets of the thirties like W.H. Auden and Stephen Spender too were of the view that art should play a subsidiary role. Auden and Spender who had solidarity with the left orthodoxy, utilized art for giving shape to their own concept of poetry. The rhetorical devices employed by them, thus became their new form of poetry—creating a new space during the thirties. There is a striking difference between Eliot and the poets of the thirties. Art is a medium through which Eliot gives religion, art, myth and philosophy a new role for the preservation of cultural identity. G.B. Shaw was a propagandist. He through the instruments of art raised his voice of reason to dismantle the social evils. Even the poets of the thirties too made art play a subsidiary role for removing social disparities from the modern world. W.H. Auden and Stephen Spender with their left lineage, utilized art for championing their cause of freedom. The rhetorical devices along with the colloquial language created a new credo for the proletariat. To the poets of the thirties art is a means; a ploy to bring into focus all those forms of hypocrisy, exploitation and the cult of violence that they realistically saw during the thirties. The capitalistic designs of exploitation and hypocrisy they saw, was an outcome of the malpractices practised by the bourgeois society. In the Shavian plays, art too has been made a means of propaganda. Shaw was no less a propagandist as he saw art a great means of propagandizing his slogan of welfare and emancipation. Shaw had raised his voice of sanity by realistically exposing the social evils prevailing in the contemporary society. Prostitution, poverty, slum-dwelling, pseudo-socialism, exploitation, violence and many such social issues which were raised by Shaw, the realist. Such realistic exposition of social evils shows how he yoked art for the purpose of propaganda. The naturalists, on the contrary to the belief that art is subsidiary, opined that art should be allowed to flourish with all its possible ways.

W.B. Yeats was one of the greatest leaders of the Irish Literary Revival at the end of the nineteenth century. While writing his early poetry, he believed that the key to true poetic creativity lay in liberating art from the shackles of age and life but in his later poetry, Yeats like Eliot became realist and wrote the poetry of ordinary things in a more sardonic vein believing that "there's more enterprise in walking naked".[4] Stephen Spender, who was a great poet and critic, came in association with the poets of the thirties, W.H. Auden, Day Lewis, and Macneice. While Yeats was writing his early poetry, he had shown proclivity to the socialistic reason of employing a language; a vitriolic rhetorics that attacked the social injustices of the capitalistic pattern of society in which the people of the lower middle classes had hardly any space to define the self. But there was a marked change in the tone and tenor in their poetic action. With the rise of the materialistic and scientific growth Yeats' bewilderment knew no bounds. Yeats in his later life did not identify himself with the modern civilization. Feeling himself badly struck with the colossal growth of the scientific paradise, he looks around and finds nowhere to go except to the city of Byzantium where he could no more be tormented by the mundane and the illusive realistic society. In "Sailing to Byzantium", Yeats' usage of symbols are suggestive of his disillusionment with the realistic society. He rather finds the modern world caught up in the sensual music." On the other hand, the world Eliot exposes in the illusive realistic society, looks pale and lacklustre giving him no hope of redemption. The symbols like cactus, stone and the heap of broken images employed in *The Wasteland*, offer no hope of redemption to man, says Eliot. Yeats drew inspiration from many a sources. For him folklores and the Celtic civilization were some of the sources which cast magical spell on Yeats. Maud Gonne was another great impact which had shaken him up right from the beginning of his poetic career. After being old and 'decrepit', he looks around and finds nothing to cling to. He throws his glimpse to the outside world having nothing to select for the subject of his poetry. Yeats introspects, looks within and comes to realise that nothing is left in him except aesthetic emotion of multitude which lay deep-seated in him. Yeats hence feels the pulsating throb of the self and comes to realise how the infrastructure and raw material drawn from within his own self could provide fire and brimstones for the hearth of his poetry. For Yeats art and the Celtic culture are inter-related with each other. Art after all, says Yeats, should be made the basic condition for speeding up and accelerating the poetic process, which gave sustenance to Yeats' poetry. It was a glorifying impact of the Celtic Movement, the Irish folklores and his early romances that gave momentum to his poetic vision. In both the phases of his early and later poetry, Yeats had created the characters like Hanarhan, Sphinx, Cuchulain, demons and fairies and all those feelings of nostalgia which make him cling to his Irish background and to his manifold iota of the self. But at the fag end of his life when he is 'old' and 'decrepit' he looks around the modern world where he finds the younger generation 'caught up' in the sensual music; he finds nothing worth-taking for the subject of his poetry. Yeats hence introspects, looks within and comes to realise that it is the third dimension of the aesthetic emotion that alone could enable him to rise up and ascend to the ivory tower where he would no more be threatened by the realistic illusive society. Yeats was critical of the modern civilization which to him, is alien to demands and bemoanings of the self. An escape to the holy city of Byzantium, says Yeats, could cater to the bemoanings of the self. Yeats' another poem, "Byzantium" is a sequel to "Sailing to Byzantium" in which art has been shown as a condition for preparing the turf of culture. The standard of art, says Yeats, can be contra distinguished with the 'unrefined' and 'unpurged'; the image of 'mind' and 'blood' is suggestive of how art is contra distinguished with the unpurged human condition. In his another poem, "Second Coming", Yeats apprehends the emergence of a new savage culture which could upturn the decent world. The imminence of a more brutal and savage culture, is perceived by virtue of a revelation. The vast images out of the "Spiritus Mundi" become part of his consciousness making him aware of the arrival of a more savage culture which could threaten the moral, ethical, social and aristocratic values in which "mere anarchy is loosed upon the world". Yeats writes:

> When a vast image out of Spiritus Mundi
> Troubles my sight: somewhere in sands of the desert
> A shape with lion body and the head of a man.[5]

Matthew Arnold in an identical way realizes how the lack of moral force during the later part of the Victorian era, could take man to 'anarchy'. Yeats again projects himself as a disillusioned angry young man finding himself a great misfit in the modern age. Yeats writes:

> There is no country for old men. The young
> In one another's arms, birds in the trees
> Those dying generations...at their song,[6]

The moderners, says Yeats, have thus no inkling of the heritage and the root they belong to. The civilization, says Yeats, undeniably passes through different phases of the humanistic, intellectual and economic processes. But at the same time Yeats gives topmost priority to the upbringing of culture, refinement, elegance and aristocratic values what Eliot attributes them to the 'elucidation and correction of taste'. Therefore art, says Yeats, is the epicenter of self-realization. In his poem, "Sailing to Byzantium", he finds the modern world soulless having no propensity of beauty and creativity. The sea-images like fish and fowl are suggestive of the lack of moral and spiritual order. Shakespeare's *Macbeth* opens with the convulsion of the moral and ethical order in which Yeats finds himself a great misfit. To Yeats society devoid of the aristocratic, ethical, moral and artistic values cannot cater to the aesthetic emotion. Such colossal growth of the realistic society devoid of art, perception and creativity, says Yeats, would take man to nowhere but to spiritual barrenness. Likewise Eliot opines that the endless growth of intellect and the scientific facts lead to the realistic illusive society. Yeats, on the other hand, contemplates of escaping to the city of Byzantium with renunciation. As escape to the city of Byzantium says Yeats, alone can purge him of his spiritual sickness. Yeats is after all a perfectionist knowing nothing of the compromise through which he could make his life worth-living. Every addition of the materialistic and scientific progress man has achieved so far, says he, would take him nowhere but to the endless labyrinth of loneliness. As such being aware of the spiritual sickness in the midst, he calls upon the holy sages to consume his spiritual sickness. In the "Second Coming" Yeats undergoes a state of revelation and becomes aware of the spiritus mundi through which he perceives the emergence of a savage culture that could threaten the finer sensibilities, the literary, cultural, artistic and above all the aristocratic values. Yeats is realistic enough to reason his spiritual sickness finding no way out but to call upon the holy sages to "gather him into the artifice of eternity". In "Among School Children", Yeats looks into the problem of old age feeling himself old and decrepit; he attributes old age to a mocking 'absurdity'. Yeats studies the co-relation of the mind, soul and the body and philosophically explains his logistics of human life arguing that human life is a totality of the mind, soul and the body through which man can live a balanced and harmonious life. Yeats applies his precepts and logistics to unravel and define the meaning and riddle of human existence. As tree is a totality of the root, stem and the leaf, so is the human life. As such the dance cannot be separated from the dancer. In a similar way art, says Yeats, too cannot be separated from the artist; this is how Yeats applies his logistics in his concept of artistic creativity. As such the Irish and Celtic landscapes made him play a crucial role in shaping him up into a complete artist. The Celtic civilization, the Irish folklores and all those primitive and instinctual patterns always remained at the back drop of his mind, played a key role in providing him the fire and brimstone which ultimately became the infrastructure of his hearth of poetry. Maud Gonne too made an indelible imprint upon his inner mind; each and every line Yeats has written is reminiscent of his indespensable association of Maud Gonne. In Yeats' poetry there is no role of ambiguity. In other words, there is a certain degree of logistics impinged upon Yeats' poetry. Yeats basks in glory and revels in interweaving tales of Irish folklores and Celtic culture into the fabric of his stories. As such the images like Cuchulain, Hanarhan, fairies and demons—all can be seen magically spun into the tapestry of his poetry. But Yeats was disillusioned with the realistic illusive society. He could see that the realistic cult of poetry was no more relevant to cater to the aesthetic emotion. As a consequence, he could see the prevalence of a savage culture that could upturn the finer, moral, ethical, artistic and above all aristocratic values on which he had raised his hope of redemption. Yeats had staunch faith in the values generated by the Celtic culture—and all that he had seen during his childhood, was powerful enough to create in him a sense of nostalgia but at the fag end of his poetic career he felt himself very much threatened by the declining spiritual, ethical and aristocratic values. "In Leda and the Swan", Yeats symbolically probes how various cultures and civilizations were replaced by one another in the cyclical order. In the "Second Coming", Yeats foresees the emergence of a more violent and savage culture giving rise to mere anarchy and to splitting up of personality. T.S. Eliot, on the other hand, raises his voice and concern at the socialistic patterns of society that to him, could be a great stumbling block to the individual integrity. Poetry, therefore says Yeats, is truth seen with all its passion. Pronouncing his opinion upon Ezra Pound's poetry. Yeats writes, "probably too much attention has been paid to the technique of the cantos at the expense of its contents. It is because Pound's ideas and subject matter are important in themselves that poetry is living".[7] In Arnold's domain, on the other hand, poetry has been elevated to the status of religion. Modern man has been depicted as on alert man. It is difficult for him to cling to one single identity. What is striking is that Eliot's poetry is the assimilation of varied perspectives, backgrounds and forms giving rise to a new form of poetry, which could accommodate discordant voices and verisimilitude of identities. Making review of Yeats' poetry Eliot writes:

> Yeats was one of the latter. He was one of those few whose history is the history of their own time, who are

part of the consciousness of an age which cannot be understood without them.[8]

NOTES

1. William K. Wimsatt JR and Cleanth Brooks, *Literary Criticism: A Short History*, Oxford & IBH Publishing Co. Pvt. Ltd., New Delhi. Ed., 1957, p. 667.
2. Quoted William K. Wimsatt JR and Cleanth Brooks, *Literary Criticism: A Short History*, Oxford & IBH Publishing Co. Pvt. Ltd., New Delhi, ed., 1957, p. 664.
3. *Ibid.*, p. 663.
4. W.B. Yeats, *The Second Poetry*, edited with an introduction by A. Norman Jeffares, Radha Publication, Calcutta, p. 63.
5. *Ibid.*, p. 99.
6. *Ibid.*, p. 104.
7. Ezra Pound, *Selected Prose*, Faber and Faber Ltd., London, edited by William Cookson, ed. 1973, p. 7.
8. T.S. Eliot, "Yeats", *Twentieth Century View*, edited by John Unterrecker, Cliffs, N.J.J., ed., 1963, p. 63.

4

Assimilation of Identities

In Eliot's projection of identity, the moral and the spiritual aspects get synonymous with each other. Eliot differentiates between the moral and the immoral, good and evil from the biblical standpoint. In his canvas of the poetic art, characters move on with the realization that they become drifted from the mainstream life. Eliot thus exposes the directionlessness of the modern world. At the same time the colossal growth of science and intellect, says Eliot, makes a negative impact on the inner being of man. Eliot nowhere does develop the know-how of the self in which there lie the various elements of the impulse. In Eliot's dynamics of poetry voice of the inner self is ratiocinated by allowing it to pass through the aesthetic sense. What Eliot concentrates is the illusiveness of the real world. On the contrary, in the Indian mythology, the philosophy of *maya* basically says that everything that exists in the real world is illusive or is nothing but delusion. Flaubert and Eliot stand at the two different poles. Flaubert makes use of the technique of expressionism and the naturalistic flair of writing that uninhibitedly go on to reflect the aesthetic emotion. Eliot spends most of his creative energy on exposing the mushrooming growth of the mundane realities. Whatever Eliot takes note of the basic fact that man's loss of identity is an outcome of the growth of the scientific facts in the real world. The naturalistic writers like Flaubert and Oscar Wilde on the other hand opine that the doctrine of the inner self is the basic fulcrum on which the whole transaction of human life rests.

For the Naturalists the discrepancy taking place between the solipsistic and the external real world leads to the process of the splitting up of personality. Perhaps it is the dissociation of the self and the 'real' world that gives rise to the dissociation of sensibility in Eliot's domain of poetry. Eliot was on the one hand bewildered at how to form a balance between tradition and individual talent. For Eliot, tradition was more important than the individual talent. As such he seriously argues for adjusting and renewing individual talent at every existing order, for him extinction of personality and restraining the turning loose of emotion are an unavoidable necessity. Eliot was more concerned with delving deep into and grappling with the problem of identity than with exploring the aesthetic emotion. I.A. Richards in his *Principles of Criticism* elaborates the mechanism through which various impulses stir the mind. Definitely there was a deep impact of psychology that emanates from Richards' deliberation in which the impact of the play of impulse can be seen making an indelible imprint into the mind. It can however be said that whatever Eliot realistically makes exposition of the modern wasteland, is a partial and incomplete study of the problem of identity man undergoes. In "Tradition and the Individual Talent" Eliot says that every age has certain characteristics. To streamline the linear growth of intellect and urbanization, Eliot links them with tradition or sense of history for elucidation of work of art and honest criticism. Eliot neither selects nor rejects, instead, he solely interlinks and adds up those developments—social, cultural, economic and above all scientific taking place in every existing order. For Eliot, a balanced relation between tradition and individual talent is the only way to give sanity and a sense of belonging to every existing order can be maintained. In his *Notes Towards the Definition of Culture* Eliot puts emphasis on promoting the growth of culture and for art and receptiveness. A rich heritage and culture, says Eliot, are equally significant as tradition is. To ignore the role of culture for the growth of art would be an incomplete study of man and his heritage. F.R. Leavis, on the other hand, thus disagreeing with Eliot, ratiocinates and comes to realize that each and every element of the past may not necessarily be relevant to the existing order.

Eliot's usage of "let us go then, you and I,/ when the evening is spread out against the sky"[1] remains implicit in his subjective co-relatives. It can be said that a work of art cannot be analyzed and interpreted without taking into account the subjective co-relatives that lay at the root of the facade of the objective co-relatives; the images, symbols and the whole range of allusions which play a crucial role in concealing those flamboyant subjective emotions. The anguish and the feeling of loneliness explored in his poetry at length, are some of the factors constituting the 'individual talent'. The search for identity for Eliot was the need to conceal and cover up the anguish of the loneliness in order to make the subjective objective. Thus, the basic driving force behind Eliot's projection of the objective co-relative was his yearning for the 'extinction of personality'. Poetry for Eliot, hence, is not the turning loose of emotions but escape from subjective co-relatives. Eliot was therefore averse to the assimilation of the subjective emotion in a work of art. The objective co-relatives propounded by Eliot thus enable him to evoke those discordant, varied and manifold discursive voices of the self. What can basically be argued is that the perception implicit in the personal and subjective experiences go on persisting as the infrastructure and scaffolding of the objective co-relative. As Eliot's admiration for and proclivity to classical learning principally projected himself to be a classicist, it can thus logically be argued is that he intends to carve out a balance between knowledge and experience. What is striking is that if personal experience for Eliot is the primary perception of an artist, his usage of the objective co-relative is the secondary; an extended metaphor of the personal and the subjective emotions existing beneath the surface of a work of art. Eliot feels nowhere the need of giving priority to the immediate experience. The personal feelings and the immediate experience which Eliot cooks up in his private workshop of poetry, are thus necessarily are an outcome of his subjective feeling that exist at the grass-root level. Eliot walks up alone with all those feelings of anguish and loneliness which he assimilates in his private workshop of poetry. The logic behind inventing the technique of object co-relative is to put up those feelings of anguish and despair on to the mantle of his private workshop of poetry was the need to co-relate them with those feelings of utter dejection and pessimism in an objective way. It is in this sense that Eliot owes a lot to F.H. Bradley for his emphasis on self-fulfilment. Eliot like F.H. Bradley says that a work of art cannot achieve transcendence unless it concentrates on the inertia of the self. As Eliot was deeply rooted in the American tradition, his poetry explores the currents and cross-currents of the homelessness of American people. Hence, Eliot's usage of objectives co-relative basically intends to conceal and cover up the anguish and the pain of loneliness that Eliot would have himself experienced. Eliot inescapably on the subjective plane is aware of the voices that embroiled him in despair and twilight vision. The logic behind Eliot's objective co-relative is basically to find a way out to giving voice to the anguish and dilemma he had felt from within. It can however be said that his projection of "The Individual Talent" is a sum total of all his feelings of dejection, loneliness and above all of the subjective co-relatives which might have inspired him to make them interwoven into the texture of his poetic art. The symbols and images taken from Baudlair, Laforgue and Dante make his texture of poetry more enriched and complete. In his early poetry, Eliot gives vent to all his anguish and despair that make a nostalgic effect upon the reader. Eliot's "You and I" evoked in him an upsurge for creating a sense of belonging. His search for belonging, as such, becomes more intense and tragic in his great poem, "The Wasteland", the tone and tenor, the images, allusions and symbols employed in his later poetry become more embittered and sharp. In his later poems like "Ash Wednesday" and "Four Quartets", Eliot seeks affirmation of faith striking a balance between tradition and individual talent. The problem before Eliot was how to interpret and see where his root actually lay in the realistic society. What Eliot poetically endeavors is to seek various ways and means to formulate mechanisms; and resolves to defuse the dilemma and the ambivalence emanating from the subjective co-relatives.

Scrapping the disagreement of ideas through the mechanism of the objective co-relative, he projects discursive ideas and images assimilating them with the larger identity and searching for the ultimate identity.

Eliot's technique of objective co-relative does not need to be taken on the literal plane. Many a scholars have ironically interpreted Eliot's usage of objectivity on the literal plane. It calls for why Eliot emphasized the need to put objective co-relative or a set of images or a sequence of situations onto the mantle of his private workshop poetry. It can however be said that the twilight vision which Eliot might have experienced made him undergo the subjective emotion. Yeats terms it as 'multitude of emotion' enkindling an urge in the artist to make it interwoven into the texture of his poetry. As such, the two Eliot's "You and I" are the two irreconciliatory parts of the self which emerge their head in exercising the stance of the agitating self. In W.B. Yeats' "Spiritus Mundi", the panorama of the canvas on which his images, symbols and vehicles of rhetoric emerge, carry within the twilight vision which reflects from his early poetry. This poetic infrastructure, which is part of his private workshop poetry assimilates all those areas of perception concealing those emotion of despair. Thus, the need to camouflage his twilight vision receives impetus from those emotions which tend to be subjective and personal. Therefore, it is in the fitness of things to scrape the heterogeneous ideas which create conflict and disharmony on the subjective plane. In other words, the symbols, allusions and vehicle of expression built up to create the art of ambivalence enable him to project his subjective and personal experiences on impersonal plane. Varied identities get submerged into one ultimate identity. It is the search for ultimate identity which Eliot basically aspires for. In "Ash Wednesday" Eliot's search for ultimate identity reflects from are discursive experiences. In "Ash Wednesday", Eliot writes: "I don't hope to turn again",[2] shows how he urgently needed to cling to his sense of belonging. It was this search for belonging, which made V.S. Naipaul undertake his journey in order to dig up the past. The agony of unknotting the threads of identity basically provides impetus to have a comparative account of both sides of the Atlantic. Naipaul remains caught up into the web of the enigma. In his novel *Enigma of the Arrival*, Naipaul nowhere sees his enigma of life unravelled. He endlessly with ant-like business goes on to play with the riddle of life. He rationalistically goes on to argue exploring the areas of the darkness which he comes across. Like Naipaul, Eliot cultivates hope and affirmation of faith in his later poetry particularly in his "Ash Wednesday" and "Four Quartets". From this standpoint, it would be futile and illogical to say that Eliot was a wanderer. Both Naipaul and Eliot undertake journey from pillar to post. What is striking is that Eliot is no escapist as he realistically believes that the pulsating beat of the self cannot allow man to escape from the mundane world. His throbbing of the self goes on to haunt Eliot even after shifting from the domain of America to that of British Isles. Eliot does not allow prevalence of those basic, primitive, rudimentary and throbbing of the self in a work of art that goes on being part of the phantasmagoria. In "The Family Reunion", Eliot presents the mystery of the metaphysical forces that too shape up the paradox of human life. Harry suffers from illusion of committing the guilt and shows how it menacingly goes on to be a nightmarish experience. S.T. Coleridge however differentiates between fancy and imagination. Eliot's carving out the objective co-relative and usage of allusions, symbols and images—is not the end of imagination. Instead they symbolically with all their subjectivity project Eliot's vastness of poetic imagination. Eliot's dynamics of symbolism and vehicle of alliterative technique is not an end but a means to project his varied and discursive experience; conflict and dilemma and other various moods of despair and melancholy which essentially emanate from his poetic imagination. The new tone and tenor of poetry nonetheless, is evocative of the varied currents and cross-currents that he camouflages the assimilation of varied identities, backgrounds, perspectives as well as the emotion of despair and melancholy.

In Eliot's poetry, it is the assimilation of varied identities which brings about a sea-change in the new man's vision. Each and every fragment of identity built within Eliot's parameter of poetry is an outcome of the sea-change perceived in the psyche of the modern man. Eliot's "The Burial of the Dead" evokes the dissipation of the Austro-Hungarian aristocracy before 1914 and the linguistic and ethnological confusion of the post-war Europe. It can however be said that the linguistic and ethnological confusion are a direct outcome of the decay of the Romantic world of the Austro-Hungarian aristocracy existing before 1914. As such splitting up of personality in Eliot's connotation of poetry precedes to the complex assimilation of identity; cultures and the pattern of life after 1914 can be regarded in Eliot's terminology as 'heap of broken images'. 'London' is unrealistic; Madam Sostrosis is the every women of "The Wasteland". "London" has been regarded as an unrealistic city in which Lill, Albert, Eugenides, the typist and the Thames daughters can be seen with all their rootlessness and ethnological confusion. It is on account of the discordant elements of the identities which give a new tone and tenor to the modern search for identity. The lack of communication phonology and the requisite language to communicate—is something lacking in their being. Their inability to have a sense of belonging is thus part of the decay of the pre-1914 Romantic world. "The Hollow Men" tragically fail to project a rhetorical device and a meaningful language to find communion with each other. They are 'a head piece filled with straw', V.S. Naipaul in an identical way through his fictional art tends to look back, dig up the past and looks at the present the way he is built up with. Naipaul seems to stride up on the two boats. He feels himself caught up in between varied cultures, roots and perspectives. In the African and the Canadian literature, the new settlers find themselves in a great agony. A new settler having his feet stridden, feels his self caught up amidst various cultures, milieu and perspectives with a new sense of belonging. In his *Enigma of Arrival*, Naipaul feels himself caught up in a dilemma. Naipaul revels in caricaturing and presenting situations tinged with both irony and humor. Naipaul spends his energy in unravelling the knots of the enigma of human existence. His inner mind remains embroiled in solving the riddle of life. Naipaul's characters do not look back with anger instead they caricature, imitate, argue and cut jokes with a view to unravelling the knots of their identity. Having his feet settled in the alien surroundings is not, says Naipaul, the end of imagination. The need to delve down deep into the multitude of various identities, races and cultures from the socio-political, anthropological and ethnological perspective, creates an urge in him to come out of the linguistic and ethnological confusion. Both Eliot and Naipaul bring to their art of receptiveness of mind to explore the discordant and varying notes of music. The rootlessness and cultural degeneration thus always remain at the back of their mind. In "The Wasteland" and "Hollow Men", Eliot exposes the spiritual sterility. Flaubert unlike Eliot is conscious of the self. He gives priority to the throbbing of the self before putting up his stance of life in the external world. Eliot makes no conscious effort to conceal the factors responsible for the colossal growth of the human mind in the 'real' society. Eliot on the one hand links up the assimilation of the identities with the colossal growth of the 'real' world, D.H. Lawrence on the other hand searches for a new morality to find new horizons that could widen and pitch fork man with a better understanding of the text. As a result the new critics unlike Eliot were not pre-empted with analyzing poetry with all the objective co-relatives that make poetry impersonal. Eliot was pre-occupied with the ethos that in his opinion enriches art and literature at every existing order. Though F.R. Leavis was a disciple of Eliot, yet he gives a new turn and twist to the contemporary tenets of criticism which were very much influenced by Eliot and his followers. As Eliot's poetry is a by product of Ezra Pound's precision, simplicity and accuracy applied in prose. F.R. Leavis too finds his roots somewhere in Eliot's elaboration of criticism. Frontiers of criticism says F.R. Leavis cannot be kept barricaded and limited to the sense of history and the sense of tradition. From F.R. Leavis' standpoint, the true relevance of criticism remains inherent in drawing up and defining the 'producible text'. Both Pound and Eliot show distrust of democratic tendencies in politics. Many a contemporary problems which are product of the social problems emanating from the cultural standards. In 1932, a new cult of imitating Eliot arose. Political and economic forces at work demanded new poets to emerge on the literary horizon and tackle the problems emanating from Eliot's pre-emptive bid of maintaining cultural standards. It is indicative of the basic fact how Eliot's bafflement knew no bounds at Man's cultural aberration on account of the fear existing on the psychic plane. Criticism says F.R. Leavis should be made intelligible to intellectuals on general interpretation of tradition and historicity. Miss Weston in her book *From Ritual to Romance* applies mythological study of the symbols and images employed by Eliot. F.R. Leavis on the other hand in his numerous books of criticism makes morality an integral part of the frontier of the criticism. F.R. Leavis castigates Eliot for putting up too much obscurity that becomes a stumbling block to the reader's comprehension. Christopher Caudwell unlike Eliot and the new critics gave new meanings and dimensions to the analysis of a work of art. Caudwell's tenets of criticism is based on social criticism when a work of art is put to the spur of criticism from the sociological perceptive. With the emergence of the new sociological order, a work of art says Caudwell needs to be analyzed and seen from the sociological perspective. It would not be out of place to pin-point poets like W.H. Auden and Stephen Spender who sociologically argued for creating a new solidarity by their proclivity to the left orthodoxy. Caudwell's canon of social criticism, unlike Eliot's, neither takes into account the sense of history nor the ambiguities that prompted Empson to explore the most difficult meaning out of meaning. Caudwell instead, resorted to a new kind of social criticism in which social strata too gave new innuendoes and insinuations of meanings. In his remarkable essay "Poetry and Science" Richards plays the role of a new critic putting emphasis on knowing the new form of experience. Richards is artistically concerned with seeing how each and every tenet of poetry makes impact upon the reader.

The problem of identity dealt within the domain of Eliot's poetry is a by product of assimilation of identities that makes man stand at a crossroad. As modern poetry is complex, obscure and multidimensional, the problem of identity operative in Eliot's poetry is multilayered and manifold. The basic reason, says Eliot, behind the splitting up of personality is not the mere loss of identity instead it is rather the assimilation of identities into a new identity which remains persistent and pervasive beneath the surface of Eliot's exploration of the modern life, takes place on a canvas on which assimilation of identities gives a new dimension to man's hankering after the illusive life. Therefore, it is not merely the loss of identity instead it is the assimilation of varied identities which brings a sea change to the modern living. Eliot's bewilderment realistically lay in grappling the problem of the inbuilt process of assimilation of identities in which the discordant elements of identities play a crucial role in making man undergo in a fix. Thus, the pursuit of knowing identity of the modern Wasteland is the basic driving force which makes man run after his identity. What is striking is that Eliot's hearth of poetry explores assimilating identities to know man's search for his belonging. Identity in Eliot's exploration of poetry undergoes change and assimilates them leading to a new identity. Concept of assimilation of identities gets further enhanced and clarified when Eliot in his essay, "Tradition and the Individual Talent", logically argues for the intermingling of the past with the existing order—provides the turf for assimilation of varied identities, cultures, milieu and backgrounds into a new identity. As Eliot was conscious of the discordant elements of identities—racial, political, socialistic and cultural, he essentially felt the need to invent a new kind of rhetoric that could accommodate and adjust varying modes of identities. Perhaps, Eliot is one of the saddest poets of the modern age. His melancholy and despair as such can be felt on taking into account of his need to accommodate both sides of Eliot, "You and I" into a balanced harmony. Right from his early poetry, his despair and melancholy was evident; a patient lying etherized on the table in a half conscious state—is indicative of the need to give vent to those melancholic experiences and moods of despair which emerge into the inner flux of his mind by virtue of those assimilating identities which created melancholy and despair in him. In the Nehruvian philosophy, no such assimilation of identities takes place. Each and every component of the composite culture, says Nehru, has its own identity. But each and every integral of the composite society falls into the mainstream of the Nehruvian concept of cultural harmony, varied identities—racial, cultural even political, fall into the mainstream of the composite society. E.M. Forster's depiction of the problem of identity is no less important than Eliot's. Forster realistically brings into focus all those problems emanating from the racial, cultural and religious and socio-political identities. Forster's way out to grapple the problems which were an outcome of the conflict taking place on the racial, cultural and religious planes lies in creating a common passage where people of varied cultures and races could live with dignity and self-respect. In the Forsterian world, no such assimilation of identities takes place. Varied cultural identities remain existent with all their problems. For each and every character identity is the most crucial problem. It is identity which becomes the sole reason of the conflict operating within the psyche. In Forster's art of fiction, no assimilation of identity takes place. The hope of harmony which had provided a glimmer of hope in the mosque amounts to 'boum' in the cave. Forster seeks harmony and solace in creating a balance amongst varied identities and cultures in a passage. As Eliot was well aware of the problem of identity, he explores those discordant elements of identities that play havoc with man's inner being. Eliot knows no escape from the problems existing on the realistic plane. Unlike the romantics, he realistically brings into focus the amalgamation of varied identities into one single identity that remains persistent at the uppermost. It is in this background that all Eliot's approach to dealing with the problem of identity needs to be addressed. Forster never looks back in his depiction of the problem of identity. V.S. Naipaul on the other hand, with all his zest for seeing life, grapples with the problem of identity in order to solve the riddle of the human existence. His incessant arguments go on to prevail to search for the enigma of identity. The enigma of 'arrival' which he seeks to know is never realized into a concrete destination. The riddle of life which is intended to be solved goes on to be more complicated with every 'arrival'. His migration to the alien surroundings at the same time menacingly grips his mind to untie the knots of the riddle of identity. His escape to the alien surroundings is a place where he finds himself in a state of dilemma. The colonial, racial and above all the alien surroundings create in him assimilation of the distinct identities and cultures—compels Naipaul to look back and see how the roots which he once belonged, have undergone a sea-change. Naipaul's fiction, realistically evinces how a new settler in the alien surroundings is faced with identity crises. Likewise W.B. Yeats deals with the problem of identity in an identical way. Yeats finds no common ground between the readers and the poet. The Americans felt independent, cut off and drifting from the ethics of their tradition. As a consequence, they started experimenting new forms and meters. The old vocabulary, syntax and rhetoric had replaced the new strange allusions and symbols which are suggestive of the decay of tradition. As Eliot does not belong to a particular tradition either, two Eliots in "You and I" are indicative of the despair that might have prevailed in the inner mind of the poet. The reason why Eliot had written "Tradition and the Individual Talent" is that it was his need to co-relate the racial and ethnological problems with the sense of history and tradition. As Eliot finds 'London' an unreal city, he is concerned at the decay of tradition; his poetry basically deals with the homelessness of people showing shock and grief at the dissipation of their sense of belonging. It can however be said that Americans were responsible for experimenting complex poetry; they found themselves nowhere and non-existent as they are situated away from the Atlantic. On account of the assimilation of cultures, values and above all varied identities, they find themselves at a crossroad. The basic reason of their incessant search for identity is to existentially know where they stand. Eliot's poetry is a product of many perspectives, identities and backgrounds; assimilation of such identity says Eliot, thus has given rise to a more complicated life. It would be rather too simplistic to say that Eliot's poetry which deals with the loss of identities, became under currents of varied discordant elements and identities which remain invisible beneath the outer surface of human life, which could be felt at the psychic plane. It can, however, be said that Eliot's poetry tries to find some form out of forms. The typicality of the modern verse can be estimated from Ezra Pound's poetry. In Pound's poetry the comparison is made not for the sake of similarities but for the sake of difference. Eliot was a creation of Ezra Pound. The impact of Pound can be estimated from the basic fact how Pound had himself reviewed and edited the original draft of Eliot's *The Wasteland*. The impact of Pound thus can be seen in the selection of the syntax, symbols and rhetorical devices employed therein. Americans employed their language as if they had themselves invented it. The Americans are different from the British on account of the change of landscape and the change seen in their syntax of poetry.

Eliot lies caught up in between two traditions; the American and the British. The problem of identifying with either of two traditions—is the basic problem that makes him undergo difficult situations. In Eliot's depiction of identity, the ever growing colossal growth of intellect plays a negative role in making man spiritually disorganized. The ever growing consciousness, says Eliot, makes man lose the tether of faith. Identity in Eliot's poetry is one of the most crucial problems. Characters interwoven into the texture of his poetry, undergo a deep conflict on account of the dismantling faith. In "Love Song of J. Alfred Prufrock", the protagonist does not have the power of evocativeness of his inner being. He is a typical character devoid of the power of making proposal, passes through hundreds of revisions before making a proposal. Eliot's protagonist hardly knows the self he has from within. The foremost work for his protagonist is to look within and know the root of his existence. It can be seen how Naipaul's protagonists in identical ways fail not only in resolving the problem of their identity but also in knowing their belonging. In Alfred's love song the meaning and concept of love has undergone a sea-change. In *Portrait of a Lady* the lack of communication goes on to perverse the protagonist, the elderly lady who ironically happens to see her proposal uncommunicated. As such the problem of identity is an outcome of man's lack of communication. Love, says Eliot, is no more sacred. Eliot applies the technique of parallelism and contrast in order to see the problem of identity in its true shape and form. Eliot's *The Wasteland* opens with a note of irony. Characters in Chaucer's *The Canterbury Tales* emerge with freshness, vivacity and singing of birds. The arrival of April in Chaucer's *The Canterbury Tales*, essentially brings spiritual awakening. But April in Eliot's *The Wasteland* brings nothing but spiritual sickness and loneliness. The modern man no more has power to undertake the religious pilgrimage—is something which makes his life meaningless. Therefore, search for identity is one of the basic factors which makes Eliot's protagonist spiritually sick. His characters are thus a product of the ever-growing colossal growth of knowledge and intellect. For Eliot knowledge and ever-growing consciousness are replete with each other. Eliot keeps his eyes wide open in the real society.

Realism and Naturalism are two poles set apart in Eliot's poetry. The world Eliot creates is a by-product of the realistic cult of society keeping his eyes wide open on the ever growing conciseness of the realistic society. The technique of parallelism and contrast is the basic mechanism through which he makes exposition of the realistic world. What is striking is that Eliot's sense and sensibility remains caught up into the discordant elements of identities—racial, cultural, ethnic and religious. Eliot unlike W.B. Yeats revels in the dissociation of sensibility varied identities—racial, cultural and religious even political, get amalgamated into one single identity. "The Hollow Men" have been shown caught up in their endless arguments in a bit to know and search for their identity. Thus, technique borrowed from Laforgue helps build symbols and images in a system for communicating to man living in the metropolis. Assimilation of identities is thus what remains hidden beneath the outer surface of the ever changing realistic society. It thus can however be said that loss of identity is an indirect consequence of amalgamating identities, perspectives and backgrounds. Yeats like Eliot too shares his anguish at the dismantling of identity. In Eliot's *The Cocktail Party*, the images and symbols and above all the rhetorical devices employed therein are suggestive of assimilation of varied identities cultures and perspectives. Man, says Eliot, in spite of all his pretences to run away from the real world finds himself struck with his throbbing self. Eliot adopts the technique of objective co-relative for concealing the discordant identities which go on to remain the consciousness of his being. The problem of identity in his *The Cocktail Party* has been realistically dealt with. The amalgamation of identities is thus suggestive of the racial, ethnic and political background and perspective taking place in the real society is devoid of the aesthetic sense.

With the growth of intellect, there had been a sea-change in the nature and treatment of identities. Eliot laments at the dysfunctional mechanized realistic society. Identity in Eliot's world can be regarded as a yardstick through which man adjusts and balances his self at an existing order. Any deviation from the set values leads to deviation from the cultural and religious identity. Identity thus functions as a minaret through which a character makes resolution by defining his stance in the real world. Eliot keeps his eyes wide open on the realistic plane. Man says he is hardly aware of the doctrine of the self that gives a true identity to his character. Eliot's treatment of identity remains operative in many ways. His characters can be seen caught up in a dilemma; a web of conflict. His characters projected on the canvas always find themselves arguing endlessly. In "Love Song of J. Alfred Prufrock", the protagonist is a product of his own dilemma. He measures his problem in terms of insignificant and trivial objects. The inability to communicate to the modern man while living in the 'real' world constitutes the typicality of his problem. The proposal of love is never realized in the concrete sense. Prufrock's mind undergoes hundreds of resolutions and revisions before mustering courage to go ahead with his proposal. In *Portrait of a Lady*, it is she who takes initiative with the protagonist. Their love relationship goes on to remain finally inconclusive. In "The Wasteland", "Gerontion" and "The Hollow Men", the identity-crisis goes on to prevail at the root of the problem. Various races, cultures, identities and voices get amalgamated into one. Their search for identity reaches a point of a no return. Nothing can bring redemption to the modern man as he has severed links with their identity. It is the identity to which Eliot's character tends to cling. Eliot admires Dante simply because in his *The Divine Comedy* various cultures and civilizations fall into the mainstream of the society. There is no discord and conflict in a various cultures and civilizations operating on the socio-economic and the ethnological planes. Eliot looks back with a sense of nostalgia to revive tradition, history and myth. 'April is the cruellest month'—this is how the modern man goes on to remain wrapped up in a state of spiritual sickness. Eliot's usage of symbols and images are of Laforgue's stock; suggestive of the conflict dilemma and anguish which remain deep-seated into the psyche of the modern man. Eliot was really influenced up to a great extent by Matthew Arnold as well.

Even after the publication of *The Wasteland* in 1922, its intricacies and obscurity go on to obfuscate the reader long after its publication in 1922, Eliot's "The Wasteland" and his major poems go on to remain obscure and complicated. Eliot had submitted the original draft of "The Wasteland" to Ezra Pound. It was Ezra Pound who had applied his logistics to make it more comprehensive keeping in view of the obscurity and assimilation of various backgrounds and multiplicity of ethos and cultures. Eliot on the one hand keeps his eyes concentrated on the real world. Applying the technique of parallelism and contrast, F.R. Leavis on the other hand, gives no answer to the elucidation and correction of taste. Leavis seeks to underline only those elements of the past, which are relevant to the present. Taking into account of the inertia of the self, says Eliot, poetry is not a turning loose of emotion; overflow of powerful and spontaneous emotions would be a violation of the principle of objective correlatives. Eliot and Flaubert stand at two different poles. For Flaubert, having awareness of the mechanism and the way it functions from within, is the first priority to build one's stance of life in the real world. It is spur of harmony between the self and the real world, says Flaubert, which splits up personality. All Eliot's exposition of the real world is a consequence of the endless growth of humanism. Characters projected on Eliot's canvas of poetry, have been shown lacklustre moving meaninglessly in the real world. I.A. Richards has regarded Eliot's *The Wasteland* with music of ideas. Here the music employed in poetry has been linked up with meaning. Eliot terms it with auditory imagination. His poetry is thus reflective of the multitude of identities—religious, ethnic, anthropological. W.B. Yeats on the one hand explores the multitude of emotion, Eliot on the other hand explores the multitude of diverse identities. Eliot goes on to remain wrapped up in despair and melancholy. Tennyson had tragically explored the emotion of melancholy, grief and despair. He was at pains on account of the personal loss, which had really struck from within. Eliot too had raised hope on Tennyson's 'tears' and melancholy, it shows how he had looked at life optimistically. As Eliot's poetry is a totality of the multitude of identities—racial, political, religious and even anthropological; it remains mixed up in one identity. It is the amalgamation of identities, perspectives and diverse attitudes that goes on to remain jumbled with one another. Eliot's applicability of dissociation of sensibility thus lies in the mingling of diverse cultures, identities and perspectives.

Eliot was not only a critic of literature but also a critic of the declining social and cultural standard of life. He acquired British citizenship in 1927, which was confirmed by the Church of England. Eliot's views on sociological and cultural aspects have been widely dealt with in his works like, *Thoughts After Lambeth* (1931), *After Strange Gods* (1931); *The Idea of Christian Society* (1939), *Notes towards Definition of Culture* (1948), Eliot says that the larger is the degree of objectivity, the larger is the degree of perfection in him as an artist. The role of a perfect critic, says Eliot, has essentially to be objective and impersonal. In his essays on Baudlair, Eliot draws impetus from Hulme; in the light of those absolute values, man himself is judged to be essentially limited and imperfect. He is endowed with original sin. He can occasionally accomplish acts which partake of reflection as he can never make himself perfect. Ezra Pound, who had exercised great influence on Eliot, became his master, Pound who was well-versed with the literature of

Japan, Italy and France played a great role in arranging the thought and contents in a chronological order, Eliot had presented in "The Wasteland". Eliot who was baffled at the intermingling of the multitude of various identities sought for bringing those diverse experiences in a discipline, which he himself had realized. Eliot was of the view that Pound did not create the poets but he created a situation in which for the first time there was a modern movement in poetry. As a consequence English and American poets collaborated, knew each other's works and shared their culture, ethos and heritage with each other. Therefore, Pound did not create poets instead he created a situation in which both the American and the English poets collaborated with each other creating a new common heritage. In the *Selected Essays*, Eliot criticizes Arnold for his regarding literature as a substitute for religion. He is critical of Arnold holding him responsible for making culture a substitute. Eliot says that there is a possibility of interrelationship between religion and art but if culture is elevated to religion, then anarchy of feeling dominates religion in elevating culture to the extent of religion. As a consequence the phenomenal experiences like aesthetics, and religion become operative in society, many a great critics like Vincent Buckley and F.R. Leavis have pointed out at some of the limitations of Eliot's art of poetry. Vincent Buckley in his essay, *Poetry and Morality* holds the view that Eliot regards emotion inferior to thought and feeling. He finds ambivalence and ambiguity in his treatment of emotion in the poetic process. The purpose behind evolving the objectives co-relative, says Vincent Buckley, is to avoid any direct emotion in his poetic experience. It is Eliot's priority to thought than to feeling makes him regard Dante superior to Shakespeare. In his essay, "Tradition and the Individual Talent", Eliot draws a line of demarcation between the man who suffers and the artist who creates. The role of a poet, says Eliot, is similar to that of a medium of escape from personality and subjective emotion—is thus indicative of the basic fact that propositions from the objective co-relative are an outcome of the same identity.

F.H. Bradley firstly expresses his vision of his life in terms of perfection. Perfectionism is a state of vision in which it is expressed by the immediate experience. Secondly, perfectionism comes out of the thought and reality. But in such a situation F.H. Bradley's immediate experience and perfection become close to each another. What is striking is that according to F.H. Bradley's vision there are situations which are not covered and catered by thought and reality. Whatever is elaborated by the empiricists, perfectionism is an original state which lies outside the qualities—says Bradley, constitutes the immediate experience. Eliot was an ardent admirer of F.H. Bradley. He attributes his writing to 'perfectionist style'. F.H. Bradley says that the empiricist vision may not cater to perfection and originality as they contemplate everything in terms of experience or whatever lies deep-seated in their mind.

As Edmund Wilson (b. 1895) was well versed in German, French and Russian cultures. He applied the comparative method to understand the trends of the cross-cultural society. Wilson had review Eliot's For Lancelot Andrews. Wilson was firm in his reviewed of Eliot's *For Lancelot Andrewes*. Wilson was firm in his review of Eliot's *For Lancelot Andrewes* as he did not retreat whatever he had said earlier on Eliot. Eliot had opined that "It is doubtful weather civilization can endure without religion",[3] whereas Wilson answered firmly; "We have got to make it endure."[4] Eliot puts emphasis on objective co-relative in order to create objectivity whereas Wilson stresses the need of ontological criticism. Wilson is a cultural critic who assesses a writer's write-up taking into consideration the conditions which shape him up. Eliot on the other hand criticizes Middleton Murry for his emphasis on taking into account all those conditions which might have played a significant role in making William Wordsworth write Lucy poems while creating a work of art. Eliot on the other hand takes it unnecessary for he wholly puts up the paraphernalia of objective co-relative to be modus operendi to form objectivity. Edmund Wilson like Allen Tate takes into consideration all those factors and conditions which play a significant rule in forming a writer's ideas. Tate's "Tension in Poetry", Winter's pseudo—reference and Empson's seven types of ambiguity gave various shades and designs of new criticism. Eliot was thus a new harbinger of cross-cultural perspective which could cut across various cultures and societies. While elaborating the right use of poetry Eliot writes "The most useful poetry, socially would be one which could cut across all the present stratification of public taste—stratifications which are perhaps a sign of social—disintrigation".[5] Herbert Read while reviewing Eliot's poetry says that there is more imagism than in Pound's poetry. Herbert Read writes: "Mr. Eliot in his introduction to the acuteness—the acuteness of the athlete who has to run the same course."[6]

F.R. Leavis through his "Scrutiny" proves the common and linking factors which connect the existing order to tradition. Leavis from this aspect can be regarded as more Elioton than Eliot. In his another essay, "A Note to the Definition of Culture", Eliot puts emphasis on the significance of culture, taste and polish. From Eliot's point of view, larger is the degree of cultural awakening in a work of art the larger is the degree of taste, refinement and creativity. With the rise of the vehicle of the mass media, a new cultural renaissance, says Leavis, has moved the masses. The on-going transference of communication and information, says he, draws attention to the need of morality. From Leavis' standpoint, in his various books like *The Common Pursuit* and *The Great Tradition* he could be seen in a new role of giving feedback to the common masses. What Leavis means to say that it is the faculty of morality that can identify the relevance of the existing order to tradition, Leavis leaves no ambiguity in between the existing order and tradition. D.H. Lawrence in his novels like *Sons and Lovers* and *Women in Love* discusses the impact of the arrival of a new culture on account of the growth of scientific facts. In *Sons and Lovers*, he develops a new form of knowledge in which the emergence of the realistic society acts as a new variable for probing and understanding the new situation and plight of man. Paul, Clara and Mirriam—all are projected as a product of the arrival of the new industrialized culture in which they find themselves a great misfit. Lawrence draws attention to the enormity of intellect which leads to the cropping up of new values ingrained in the new commercialized society. Art for Eliot is thus an assimilation of the present and the past. Without the sense of involvement of history, art, says Eliot, cannot come into existence. Art for George Orwell on the other hand is related with the sense and sensibility of the lower middle classes. Shaw soon found himself fed up with the Fabian society. He had raised high hopes from the Fabian culture but soon he got himself disillusioned with whatever promises of emancipation of the lower middle classes were made. Shaw thus came to realize that the altruistic plans made by Fabian culture was of no avail. Both Orwell and Eliot adopt identical measures to retain the individual integrity. In Eliot's poetry it is the inertia of the self which gives impetus to the subjective feelings. He applies his logistics through his private workshop of poetry to explain his aesthetic verse. What is striking is that Eliot aesthetically rationalizes emotion. He rather invents a paraphernalia of giving feedback to the aesthetic self. As a matter of fact, Eliot allows his verse to pass through the aesthetic emotion in order to keep the individual integrity intact. Both Eliot and Orwell gave priority to the restoration of individual integrity. Eliot had applied the mechanism of objective co-relative to restrain and cover up the raw emotion. Years spent in Boston really haunted and recuperated Eliot's mind. Americans lived away from the Atlantic, invented a new vocabulary and thought patterns bearing a great tenacity to absorb the shock treatment meted out to the typical American culture. They have a great propensity to ignore the past as if nothing were done wrong to them. What is striking is that they project too much novelty in order to renew and re-live with a new set of human situations. Arthur Miller, Sylvia Plath, Earnest Hemingway and Emily Dickinson—all present and depict various modes and attitudes of the American cross-cultural society. Americans rather have great propensity to accommodate and adjust themselves in the given trends and situations. American poetry is the poetry of freedom giving man no opportunity to look back, see and review what had suddenly and unexpectedly come upon them. Sylvia Plath and Emily Dickinson were conscious of the American ways of living in which they found themselves a great misfit. As such Eliot had no option but to concentrate on aesthetic emotion. Americans revelled in their fragmentariness whereas Eliot prefers to look back and assimilate the ethos and culture and above all the past and present whatever aesthetic self he had. Eliot on the one hand with great passion and force applies the dynamics of objective co-relative. But the inner motif of applying the objective co-relative is basically directed to keep the individual integrity intact. Orwell in an identical way applies the code of double speak in order to retain the individual integrity. Orwell was averse to the dictatorial and the totalitarian powers as they relentlessly did whatever they could have done to distort the 'history'. Eliot retains his individual integrity in adhering to the rich heritage, culture ethos and above all to the exuberance of the human spirit. Leavis on the other hand comes to realize growing popularity of the sources of mass media right from the 50s and 60s. He apprehends that people addicted to reading or whatever is printed and published by the vehicles of mass media, may deviate them from the right use of frontiers of criticism.

Eliot was bewildered at the pace with which the decline of cultural standard inundated the socio-cultural fabric of society. He came to find the contemporary indigenous society fragile and vulnerable to its exposure to the intracultural interaction. The exposition of the realistic society he makes, presents a bleak scenario in which the intracultural modes of living with their manifold and diverse propositions, get interacted. The phenomenal experiences like clash culture thus makes a direct impact upon the behavioral patterns of man belonging to diverse culture and identities. With the emergence of the global culture, a cross-cultural perspective in the modern context, needs to be seen with more insight, care and attention. The endless growth of the commercialized and industrial society hence causes more cleavage and isolation in man. Therefore, it is imperative on the part of Eliot to apply corrective measures to restrain the fall and decline of cultural and ethnological confusion. Mathew Arnold regards such deviation from the mainstream culture as 'anarchy' which cuts deep into the socio-cultural fabric of society. The cross-cultural perspective emanating from Eliot's writings, seeks to see its impact upon the society itself. Eliot writes: "the most useful poetry, socially would be one which could across all the present stratification of public taste—stratifications which are perhaps a sign of social disintegration."[7]

A cross-cultural perspective opens up new possibilities and horizons of looking at assimilating cultures. Man living in the cross-cultural scenario as such has no way out but to receive jerks and jolts generated by the cross-cultural behavior. It is in this sense Eliot's declaring himself as a classicist, holds much water. In Eliot's exposition of the cross-cultural society, the need of spiritual anchorage becomes more poignant and sharp. The Laforguian impact hence can be seen in Eliot's usage of the symbols, images and allusions which in clear-cut way communicates to the language of the metropolis. In such a scenario where cultural aberration and ethnological confusion inundate the socio-cultural fabric of society, says Eliot, assertion of identity, as such, is another viable means through which sanity can be restored to post modern society. Richard Wright, Chinua Achebe, Joseph Conrad and Graham Greene realistically wrote about a new avalanche of identities giving rise to new areas of consciousness. Eliot in his various writings either in his plays or in poetry is always conscious of the need of assertion of identity. Identity to Achebe, on the other hand, is more important than exercise of governance; pomp and power. Black consciousness explored by Achebe highlights man's need of assertion of identity. I.A. Richard was critical of T.S. Eliot's emphasis on the aesthetic taste. Richards rather puts emphasis on the play of the psychic activities while interpreting a work of art. He takes truth to be an object of 'psychic activities' of the mind. Richards writes that 'some special mode of mental activity,[8] has been found in the pursuit of beauty. Real elucidation of a work of art, says Richards, needs to be both 'inquisitive' and 'practical' in his elaboration of practical criticism. Disagreeing with Eliot, Richards writes:

> Thus arises the phantom problem of the aesthetic mode or aesthetic state, a legacy from the days of abstract

investigation into the Good and The Beautiful and The True.[9]

NOTES

1. *Op. cit.*
2. T.S. Eliot, *Selected Poems*, "Ash-Wednesday" p. 83.
3. William Thorp, *American Writing in the Twentieth Century*, Harvad University Press, Cambridge, Massachusetts, ed., 1963, p. 298.
4. *Ibid.*
5. T.S. Eliot, *The Use of Poetry the Use of Criticism*, pp. 152-53.
6. Herbert Read, *The True Voice of Feeling*, Faber and Faber, London p. 116.
7. *Op. cit.*
8. I.A. Richards, *Principles of Criticism*, Universal Book stall, New Delhi, ed., 2002, p. 7.
9. *Ibid.*

5

Eliot and Function of the New Critics

Eliot's concept of criticism is wholly based upon impersonality. The new school of criticism propounded by Eliot is different from that of the revival of romanticism. Eliot again in the 20th century declared himself to be a critic belonging to the classical tenets. He relies too much on realism. The human condition defined in the realistic society without taking into account the aesthetic emotion which remains implicit beneath the surface of the self. He does not take into account the threadbare details of the making of the self. His treatment of the intricacies of life, thus wholly depends upon how the humanistic and scientific developments take shape in the realistic society. It can however be said that Eliot's projection of intricacies of the realistic society might be incompatible with the infrastructure of the self. It would be then exposition of the intricacies of human life which he brings out in his various poems. I.A. Richards in his *Principles of Criticism* takes into account the areas which give a fuller understanding of the self. Richards unlike Eliot pinpoints the aesthetic emotion which plays a crucial role in giving a true portrayal of the self to the fullest possible extent. Eliot on the other hand was a great traditionalist who in the beginning had scoffed at the romantic sensibility. Later he evolves a theory of criticism at length in which spontaneous and overflow of powerful feelings had no role to play in the creativity of art. As

Eliot was apprehensive of the cultural aberrations, it was imperative on the part of him to streamline ethnological and cultural norms in a system; the system which adds up and adjusts the past with the present at every existing order. Cultural behavior, says Eliot does not have a life of its own unless it is adjusted and made part of the heritage. But the instinctual patterns which remain inherent in the fabric of the self, says Richards, cannot be restrained to the fuller extent; they are bound to come up and become part of the collective behavior of the self. As such all Eliot's paraphernalia and his exposition of the modern Wasteland, might be taken to be a partial presentation of a society in which the evocativeness of the aesthetic values lies ingrained—is the basis on which the whole range of Eliot's theory of criticism has been elaborated. Eliot's school of poetry is based upon the classical tenets of criticism. In "Tradition and the Individual Talent", for example, Eliot remarks that "Poetry is not a turning loose of emotion; but an escape from emotion; it is not the expression of personality, but an escape from personality".[1] It can however be said that Eliot's poetry is a direct outcome of the currents and cross-currents of the realistic society. Eliot nowhere perceives the reason hidden beneath the infrastructure of aesthetic perception. What is striking in Eliot's poetry is the intermingling of the diverse and discordant identities—racial, political, cultural which lie superimposed into one identity, thus a realistic depiction of cultural degeneration is an outcome of the intermingling of various identities. It was, therefore, obligatory on the part of Eliot to give voice to despair that emanates from the multitude of identity. Therefore, it was imperative need on the part of Eliot to unknot the knots of the varied multitude of identity. In "The Love Song of J. Afred Prufrock", the two Eliots, "You and I" have been shown arguing endlessly; a patient lying in a half conscious state 'etherised on table',—is suggestive of the new emergence of the races, cultures and new multitude of identities which create ethnological confusion. Eliot writes;

> Let us go then you and I
>
> When the evening is spread out against the sky

Like a patient etherised upon a table;
Let us go, through certain half-deserted streets,
The muttering streets,[2]

In his play, *The Cocktail Party*, the problem of identity with its various moods of despair, conflict and dilemma, has been depicted in its multiplicity of tones and tenors of identity. The multitude of identity hidden in the modern generation makes him ethnologically confused and isolated from the main stream of the society. In *Portrait of a Lady* the problem of identity has been depicted in an identical way. Each and every character is thus seized up with his identity. It is the problem of identity which makes the modern man perplexed in many ways. Therefore, loss of identity is the basic problem, says Eliot, which creates loneliness, spiritual sickness, apathy and above all ethnological confusion in the cross-cultural society. Its varying degrees of shifting loyalties bring about a sea-change in the behavioral patterns giving a new volte-face to man. It is thus the basic change in the behavioral patterns realistically perceived in man's cultural behavior was the basic reason by virtue of which Eliot applies the technique of parallelism and contrast. Eliot writes: "No poet, no artist of any art, has his complete meaning alone. His significance, his appreciation is the appreciation of his relation to the dead poets and artists". This shows how Eliot was pre-occupied with keeping tradition the basic models that could set right the cultural aberration from myth, religion and heritage. In "Ash Wednesday", the change in perception gets manifest when he makes assertion of his faith—is indicative of the basic fact how the subjective co-relatives in Eliot's poetry are themselves a fulcrum on which his whole variety of discursive experiences moves about. Eliot was more concerned with streamlining the individual talent with tradition than analyzing a work of art to the fuller extent. His parameter of parallelism and contrast; distinction between understanding and enjoyment and his theory of objective co-relative, thus each and every shred of his critical evaluation has been made subservient to the sense of history, myth and tradition.

The end of criticism, says Eliot, is the elucidation of work of art and correction of taste. Richards co-relates poetry with science. Unlike Eliot, Richards does not talk of the 'extinction of personality' instead he applies his emotive theory by examining the working of the inbuilt human mind. Thus, the human mind, says Richards, is a system of impulses; with each new experience the impulses undergo commotion. They go on to remain disturbed unless they pass through a new experience. Poetry, says Richards, is thus representative of the balance between experience and impulses. Richards explains the system how the play of impulses evokes a new kind of experience and exposure. It is the impulses' exposure to experience or experiences which matter most to the process of creativity. The function of a critic on the other hand says Eliot is not to find 'new emotion' but to get it intermingled with the sense of history and sense of tradition. In Richards' opinion, the true function of a critic is to record how impulses get stirred up with each addition of experience to the receptacle of the human mind. F.R. Leavis who was a great disciple of Eliot, dedicated to him book after book receiving immense inspiration to give a new dimension, a twist and turn to the history of literary criticism. Eliot on the one hand in "Tradition and the Individual Talent" systematically elaborates how each existing order should be linked up with the past-ness of the past. Every existing order says Eliot has its own demands, preferences and attitudes. But it does not mean, says he, the work should be an end in itself. This is what made Eliot to keep off and relinquish subjectivity of a work of art. In Eliot's concept of criticism, the past is made co-existed with the present while handing over the treasure of knowledge and experience from one generation to another generation. Leavis on the other hand is categorical in his opinion that only those elements of the past or of tradition should be adopted and followed up by the new generations which are relevant to the needs existing in the contemporary society. Leavis practically agrees with Eliot that each and every age has its own choice and preferences. Leavis' concept of criticism is not tailor made and pre-emptive. He goes critical while opting for—what would be good or bad. It is in this aspect Leavis coins the concept of the 'producible text' as each and every shred of the past may not be conducive to the present generation. Having taken into account the diction required at every level of time, Leavis says, creates a new concept of criticism giving a new space both to the individual and society. Leavis is critical of the role played by the mass-media. It is they, says Leavis, who decide for the society what is apt or inapt for man, above all for culture and society. Leavis thus becomes more relevant by creating in man and society an urge to make 'judgment' for themselves. Leavis logically delves deep into crux of the problem by applying his logistics for developing criteria for arriving at the 'judgment' that would be good or bad for society. Leavis argues for 'scrutiny', the cultivation of taste that could create in man to see for himself what would be proper or improper. Leavis totally dislodges the role of the media which shapes up the mind for its own sake—may not be, says Leavis in the interest of individual, culture and society. Past, says he, may not necessarily be attractive to an individual in the present. Eliot on the other hand simply talks of intermingling of the past with the present at every existing order. Leavis seems to be more practical by identifying those areas of the past which are relevant to him in the present. In his numerous works, *The Common Pursuit*, *The Great Tradition* and *The New Bearings in Poetry*, he makes inquisition and 'scrutiny' the basis on which he develops 'elucidation and correction of taste'. Leavis points out at the declining taste in various spheres of life—individual, culture, society and civilization. Leavis accelerates the work of 'elucidation and correction of taste' through the vehicle of 'scrutiny' in his 'The Great Tradition' he applies the instrument of 'scrutiny' in order to identify the tradition hidden in the individual talent. In "Tradition and the Individual Talent", Eliot elaborates the system through which the heritage and ethos get linked up with every existing order. Unlike Eliot Leavis does not argue in the round about way. Before Leavis what was foremost was to identify those areas of the 'past' which is relevant to the experiences incurred at every existing order—becomes the spring board for shaping up of the multitude of individual culture and society. As such Leavis argues for infusing his logistics to differentiate between moral and immoral. Leavis is critical of the new role played by various sources of the mass-media as it plays an anchor-sheet role in catering information to the individual and society. What Leavis emphasizes is to develop and cultivate a taste for making 'judgment'. Thus, 'scrutiny', says Leavis, is the primary step by virtue of which a faculty for the 'elucidation and correction of taste' would be developed for welfare of society. It can however be said that there is more clarity in Leavis' concept of art and morality. Leavis is thus more Elioton than Eliot.

F.R. Leavis in his review *Eliot's Stature as a Critic*, points out at some of the limitations of Eliot's criticism. Delving deep into the canons of Eliot's criticism, Leavis writes: "What was not at once appearance to all of those impressed was that some of the ideas, attitudes and valuations put into currency by Eliot were arbitrary."[3] Leavis raises questions up to what extent Eliot's formulation of objectivity and impersonality would be comprehensive and practicable. Referring to Eliot's concept of a perfect critic, Leavis says the danger lies in the degree of objectivity. The larger is the extinction of personality; the larger would be the degree of perfection in a work of art. The function of a critic instead, says Leavis, is not to rely on the Aristotelian method of parallelism and contrast; instead the work of a critic is to identify the relevance of the past at a particular existing order. Leavis rather concentrates on making scrutiny whether a particular consequence of the past is relevant to the present. Eliot ignores individual talent emanating from a work of art emphasizing that the business of an artist is not to find new emotions; instead to restrain those emotions which tend to become part of the texture of a work of art. On the other hand, the work of an artist, says F.R. Leavis, is not merely to apply the traditional mode of parallelism and contrast the true function of a critic, says he, is to identify those elements of the past which are relevant to the individual in the existing order. 'The producible text' underlined by virtue of the scrutiny becomes requisite for intermingling only those elements and events of the past with the present which should be allowed to be interwoven into the texture of a work of art. There should be some criteria, says Leavis, the basis on which the whole gamut of experience both of the past and the present can be made relevant. Elucidation and correction of taste, says F.R. Leavis, can't be done unless the collective faculty by virtue of 'scrutiny' is aroused and awakened into the artist.

Eliot looks at every existing order with a new hope. He identifies the inflow of the new incoming socio-cultural values onto the human consciousness. Eliot develops a system of reasoning or ratiocination by virtue of which he creates organic unity in a work of art. Poetry of Eliot has achieved a new dimension. His poetry makes an indelible imprint upon the art of contemporary poets who emerged on the literary horizon. The New line poets had no way out but to create a new space for them. What Eliot applies is the doctrine of the inner self by making it operative from the aesthetic standpoint. It was Eliot who was first to register his disagreement with the realistic growth of society in which the aesthetic sense hardly gets space to define its stance. The early poetry during his formative years of his career is not only a realistic exposition of the society he saw during his sojourn at Boston, it is at the same time, is suggestive of his disillusionment with the realistic growth of society. Poetry written after Eliot thus gathered momentum giving a new dimension to the New line poets to unfold. The tone and tenor applied by the New line poets was a marked departure from that of Eliot and his school of poetry. Poetry after Eliot thus reflects their disillusionment with the modernist approach to life. What is bewildering to Eliot is that man while living in the modern society is inescapably conscious of the inner monologues and of those streams of consciousness—is something what constitutes his inner behavior. Escape from the interior monologues and anguish carried by it, says Eliot, makes him behave in an awkward way finding himself a misfit in the post-war society. Man projected on the canvas of Eliot's poetry comes to the surface while defining his stance in the external illusive society with a new set of behavioral patterns. Alfred Prufrock in *The Love Song* while living a cosmetic life hardly has anything in him that could translate his proposal of love into a concrete reality; he behaves awkwardly, looks back, introspects and makes revision of what he has already made up his mind to do—hardly materializes into a concrete reality. The problem with Eliot protagonist is thus how to find a co-relation between thought and action. In "Morning at the Window", Eliot traces the attribute of the cross-cultural society in which man goes on to remain un-communicated. The burden of incommunicado goes on to prevail on his consciousness making him truly lonely. He explores a cross-cultural scenario in which the 'house wives' can be seen washing breakfast plates in basement kitchens and households; they are waiting for their partners at the 'area gates'. Eliot thus gives description of spiritually lack luster faces of people passing through the streets. Empty faces of people moving in the street rather look distorted. Similarly, "The Hollow Men" are spiritually dislocated having no propensity to communicate to the fellow strangers. They live in a state of oblivion incapable of offering prayers and communion. In "Morning at the Window", Eliot writes: "and there is nobody to communicate to their aimless smile". In *Sweeney Among the Nightingales*, Eliot realistically exposes the spiritually degenerated life of the post war society steeped in perversion—projects a bleak scenario of the post war society. Eliot basically shows his concern at the purposeless life in which man has lost his propensity to rejoice his life. Sweeney known for sexual perversion and the plot hatched against him, ends up with a big fuss—suggests the meaninglessness of the modern life. Eliot compares the purposeless murder of Sweeney with that of Agamemnon. The plot of murder of Agamemnon and proposed murder of Sweeney, have striking similarities. But the plan designed to murder Sweeney symbolizes how man stands meaninglessly confused at the cross roads. Eliot writes: "When Agamemnon cried a loud,/ And let their liquid siftings fall/ To sustain the stiff."[4]

Eliot's poetry is a melting pot of identities in which diverse identities remain submerged. In his various writings—either in his plays, poetry or in critical essays, he realistically draws attention to the arrival of a new cross-cultural identity with all its inner recesses of behavioral trends and patterns. But Eliot is not apprehensive of the new assimilating cultures instead he puts emphasis on revolving a new poetic apparatus or a new modous operandi to keep those assimilating identities intact. Eliot's writes:

> I take this period to have persisted until my nineteenth or twentieth year. Being a period of rapid assimilation, the end may not know the beginning, so different may the taste become. Like the first period of childhood, it is one beyond which I dare say many people never advance; so that such taste for poetry as they retain in later life is only a sentimental memory of the pleasures of youth, and is probably entwined with all our sentimental retrospective feelings. It is, no doubt, a period of keen enjoyment; but we must not confuse the intensity of the poetic experience in adolescence with the intense experience of poetry. At this period, the poem, or the poetry of a single poet, invades the youthful consciousness and assumes complete possession for a time.[5]

T.S. Eliot neither agrees to I.A. Richards' notion that "both a passionate knowledge of poetry and a capacity for dispassionate psychological analysis"[6] are ingredients of interpretation of a work of art. In "Tradition and the Individual Talent", Eliot rightly says that every age has its own taste, preference and trends. In his another significant book *The Use of Poetry and the Use of Criticism*, Eliot takes an identical stand in which he elaborates various uses of poetry in time and space.

Eliot writes: "The uses of poetry certainly vary as society alters, as the public to be addressed changes."[7]

Eliot applies the doctrine of the inner self to explore the throbbing pulse of the self. The real tragedy says Eliot crops up in man's life when he goes hell-bent upon overtaking and ignoring his self. Milton in *The Paradise Lost* defines the meaning of hell clarifying that hell is not a particular state nor does it exist in a physical form rather dungeon of hell goes on to prevail wherever he goes. Hell, says Milton, at the same time is rather a state of perpetual torture and inflictment heaped upon man. Eliot who was a great admirer of the classical tenets of poetry, describes hell in an identical manner. In *The Cocktail Party*, Edward's plight is something similar to that of a man wrapped up in labyrinth of loneliness. It is difficult for him to come out of the agony. Wherever Edward goes, his mind remains preoccupied with the memories associated with Lavinia. He is so obsessed with her that it is difficult for him to detach himself from her Eliot writes:

What is hell? Hell is oneself,

Hell is alone, the other figures in it

Merely projections. There is nothing to escape from

And nothing escapes to. One is always alone.[8] (*The Cocktail Party*, p. 99)

In *The Cocktail Party*, Eliot explores another dimension of the cross-cultural identity. Kafka in Metamorphosis points to the belittleness of man; whereas man in Eliot's plays passes through an experience of paradox. The shocking revelation that Edward has been treated something like a plaything or like an object creates in him a feeling of otherness. He is shocked at the unprecedental reality of being left un-communicated. Lavinia leaves Edward unexpectedly making him receive lots of jerks and jolts that make him wrapped up in the pallor of incommunicado. A feeling of otherness thus surreptitiously takes possession of Lavinia making him lonely. Eliot projects the duality of experience:

You're suddenly reduced to the status of an object-

A living object, but no longer a person.[9] (*The Cocktail Party*, p. 30)

This experience of duality thus gives a new twist and turn to a new form of human plight. 'The death of the sprit', is really a horrible experience to Eliot. Edward-Lavinia relationship too crops up an identical crisis in which man finds himself caught up between the two extremes. Eliot points to the dangerous consequences inherent in the abnormal growth of the realistic society. It is the 'death of the spirit' rather than the 'death of the body' is detrimental to man and his identity. Edward unfolds his anguish of his soul at the cessation of his identity. Edwards unfold his mind evocating the anguish of his soul:

I am not afraid of the death of the body,

But this death is terrifying. The death of the spirit—

Can you understand what I suffer?[10] (*The Cocktail Party*, p. 113)

After being deserted Edward finds himself in no man's land; neither can he live with Lavinia nor can he live without her—makes him aware of the lingering loneliness he fails to cope up with. 'Hell' in Milton's *The Paradise Lost* is not the name of a place; it is rather a state of perpetual inflictment man passes through where ever he goes. He finds perpetual torture hinged upon him. In *The Cocktail Party*, Edward finds himself a dweller of hell; wherever he goes a perpetual lingering sense of loneliness takes possession of his being. Man in Eliot poetry thus cannot escape the endless trammels of loneliness—is a new definition of loneliness given on the ontological and metaphysical plane. Eliot writes:

I cannot live with her—that is now intolerable.

I cannot live without her, for she has made me incapable

Of having any existence of my own.[11] (*The Cocktail Party*, p. 112)

In *The Family Reunion*, the supernatural elements act as the third dimension. Harry is horrified at the play of the supernatural. Harry like Edward fails to 'understand' his own plight. He fails to understand the mysterious appearance of the furies. Celia in *The Cocktail Party* too ironically fails to understand her own 'delusion'. Celia says:

I don't imagine that I am being persecuted;

I don't hear any voices, I have no delusions.[12] (*The Cocktail Party*, p. 131)

Celia is always wrapped up in her own sense of loneliness. Her sudden realization of her loneliness makes her cut off and drifted from the mainstream society—is a 'revelation' about her relationship with everybody. Eliot thus draws a line of demarcation between the 'real' and the 'unreal'; 'lover' and the beloved. As Eliot was immensely influenced by metaphysics he was deeply moved by the metaphysical reality manifest in man. The post Freudian psychoanalysts are of the view that the unconscious 'hidden' into the substratum of the human mind, is itself a reality—accrues more layers of meaning and innuendoes to the being and existence. The metaphysical reality thus says Eliot alone can dispel the gripping sense of loneliness. Eliot explains various modes, forms and conditions of loneliness cropped up on account of the emergence of a new cross-cultural society. Harry feels himself frightened because of the intriguing fear imposed by the potent force of furies—is, to him no less than a 'delusion' Celia abruptly passes through. Eliot thus draws a line of demarcation between illusion and reality; loveable and 'unlovable'; 'real' and the 'unreal':

> Can we only love
>
> Something created by our own imagination?
>
> Are we all in fact unloving and unlovable?
>
> Then one is alone, and if one is alone
>
> Then lover and beloved are equally unreal
>
> And the dreamer is no more real than his dreams.[13]

In *The Family Reunion*, Eliot explores a new area of loneliness. Harry goes on to remain a prisoner of his own illusory self. Agatha dispels the confusion saying that there is an implied meaning behind the play of the supernatural. The Furies haunt Harry simply because of his delusion of committing the guilt. Eliot thus explores man's inability to escape from his throbbing self. Harry finds himself a prisoner of his own illusory guilt. He is hallucinated and tormented by his own sense of guilt. The feeling of otherness thus cropped up in him does not allow him to be in the mainstream society. Characters living around Harry hardly understand his lingering sense of loneliness as they look at him with their own set of values. Agatha clarifies how people around him try to understand each other with their limited power of understanding. Eliot like Coleridge introduces the element of the supernatural which acts as a retributive force.

Eliot reiterates 'to understand' the human predicament in which man suddenly becomes aware of his own feeling of otherness. Eliot unlike Freud is not limited to mere selection or rejection on the psycho-analytical plane, instead, he sees unified sensibility in a work of art. Treating an experience in its fragmentariness, says Eliot, would be tantamount to incomplete explanation of an idea or of an experience. Eliot projects Harry's plight and sees transcendence and fulfilment not in fragmentariness rather in seeing a particular experience at length, says he, alone can carve out organic unity.

The use of poetry, says Eliot, is subject to the change in society in time and space. Perception, preference and attitude also change with all those socio-cultural changes taking place in every existing order. Unlike Eliot F.R. Leavis puts stress on the moral factor in ascertaining the extent to which the assimilation of the incoming socio-cultural changes could be made. In his various writings like *New Bearings of Poetry*, *The Great Tradition* and *The Common Pursuit*, F.R. Leavis pin points the need of moral factor taking place in every existing order. Eliot on the other hand elaborates the right use of poetry: "The most useful poetry, socially, would be one which could cut across all the present stratifications of public taste—stratifications which one perhaps a sign of social disintegration"[14] (pp. 152-53). George Sampson systematically studies at length the age of T.S. Eliot establishing relation between criticism and culture. Sampson systematically says that various uses of poetry differ with those changes emerging in different phases of time and space. Sampson specifies that the innovative style of Dickens, Joyce, Naipaul, as well as of the West Indian writers giving rise to a new diction, rhythm and speech through their writings. Orwell's usage of double speak has created a new manner of defining his stance in the alien surroundings. E.M. Forster's usage of the Indian terms and terminologies taken from the indigenous stock of society contributes to a new assimilation as well as evolution of a new society having different behavioral patterns. The Common Wealth and post-colonial literature at length result in a considerable import of a colloquial language giving a better frame of mind to receive the stimuli and impressions prevailing in the external illusive society. Samson systematically writes that writers like Dickens, Joyce, Naipaul and other West Indian novelists "have brought a new rhythm to popular music and their cricketers a new vitality to export"[15] (p. 927). Joseph Heller's *Catch 22*, gives an inkling of embarrassing situations man finds himself beset with—gives another form of innuendo and dilemma prevailing in the modern society. Wayner Shumaker properly studies the place of art in literature at the advent of the cross-cultural society. Shumaker is conscious of complications of receptivity when logical thought processes remain dormant. In such a situation, says Shumaker, in absorbed reading, the mind tends to "submit itself to the laws of aesthetic universe as completely as universe itself permits so that relationship can be appreciated which at cooler moments, when logical thought processes are dormant would seem puzzling and inexplicable"[16] (p. 19).

E.M. Forster like Eliot apprehends the emergence of a new cross-cultural society in which man hardly feels his throbbing pulse of the self. Forster further exposes the currents and cross currents of intricacies of the multi-religious and the multi-cultural society in which people of different races and backgrounds feel themselves at a cross. In *A Passage to India*, both Aziz and Fielding come face to face in different directions bringing no common passage. Forster like Eliot thus laments at man's inability to 'understand'. Mrs. Moore in the opening scene of the novel simply says that before taking her stance she only relies on whether she admires an idea or an experience. In Eliot's domain of private workshop of poetry both 'understanding' and 'enjoyment' are complimentary to each other. Eliot opines man cannot enjoy unless he understands. Forster makes fun of Keynes' full employment in which man has no way out to live with his split up self. Forster writes: "There will be work for all and play for all. But the work and the play will be split; the work will be mechanical and the play frivolous. If you drop tradition and culture you lose your chance of connecting work and play and creating a life which is all of a piece. The past did not succeed in doing that, but it can help us to do it, and that is why it is so useful".[17] Bertrand Russell is too conscious of the dangers inherent in the abnormal growth of 'knowledge' making man entwined into the endless trammels of alienation. Being conscious of the inherent dangerous of the abnormal growth of the mind, Russell writes: "It is by no means uncommon to find men whose knowledge is wide but whose feelings are narrow. Such men lack what I am calling wisdom."[18] But at the same time Russell adds that the dangers inherent in the pursuit of 'knowledge' can be diffused by intermingling knowledge with 'wisdom'. Russell writes: "In such ways the pursuit of knowledge may become harmful unless it is combined with wisdom; and wisdom in the sense of comprehensive vision is not necessarily present in specialists in the pursuit of knowledge."[19]

Ezra Pound was the creator of T.S. Eliot. His two significant works, 'Homage to Sextus Properties' (1917) and 'Hugh Selwyn Mauberley' are the poems in which Pound portrays the currents and cross-currents of the British culture.

NOTES

1. *Op. cit.*
2. T.S. Eliot, *Selected Poems*, "The Love Song of J. Alfred Prufrock", p. 11.
3. F.R. Leavis, "Eliot's Stature as a Critic," Commentary, Nov. 1958, p. 400.
4. T.S. Eliot, "Sweeney Among the Nightingales", *Selected Poems*, p. 47.
5. T.S. Eliot, *The Use of Poetry and the Use of Criticism*, Faber and Faber Ltd., London, pp. 33-34.
6. Quoted by Eliot, *The Use of Poetry and the Use of Criticism*, p. 17.
7. *Ibid.*, p. 150.
8. T.S. Eliot, *The Cocktail Party*, Faber and Faber, London, ed., 1971, p. 99.
9. *Ibid.*, p. 30.
10. *Ibid.*, p. 113.
11. *Ibid.*, 112.

12. *Ibid.*, 131.
13. *Ibid.*, 137.
14. T.S. Eliot, *The Use of Poetry and the Use of Criticism*, pp. 152-53.
15. George Sampson, *The Age of T.S. Eliot*, The Concise Cambridge History of English Literature, Vikas Publishing House Pvt. Ltd., ed., 1975, p. 927.
16. Wayner Shoemaker, *Literature and the Irrational*, Prentice Hall Inc., ed., 1960, p. 19.
17. E.M. Forster, "Does Culture Matter?", *An Anthology of Prose*, edited by J.P. Singh, Vikas Publishing House (P) Ltd., ed., 1995, p. 40.
18. Bertrand Russell, "Knowledge and Wisdom", *Anthology of Prose*, edited by J.P. Singh, Vikas Publishing House, ed., 1995, p. 23.
19. *Ibid.*

6

A Cross-cultural Perspective

Criticism and culture are the two aspects of the same coin. The more culture is refined, polished and enhanced, the larger is its propensity to create beauty and perfection. Varied nuances of art, beauty, perception and above all creativity would manifest itself unless culture and upbringing are made to exist. Culture devoid of art lacks power of perception and creativity. Criticism sharpens the critical acumen of the artist. Karl Marx and Engels argued for creating new solidarity with the 'have-nots'. For them, only the 'have-nots' are capable of creating art, beauty and perception. Christopher Caudwell too interpreted art in terms of the aspirations of the people belonging to the downtrodden. Their approach from the socialist outlook gave rise to the bourgeois culture. Thus, a new meaning and definition of culture delineated by Marx and Engels made things upside down. Trade union and new scale of wages; the employer and the employed; exploiter and exploited—were seen with a new angle. A new literature of the working classes and the proletariat came into prominence with its widespread circulation—created a new passage and solidarity. D.H. Lawrence's 'art and morality' on the one hand argued for applying a new morality at the shift of values in the modern society. With the rise of the industrial and commercial revolution new rules were writ large; a new definition of morality with a new preferential taste and judgment. As such, a new kind of journal found their way with a new proclivity to enjoy the proletariat literature; their attitudes, preferences, sex and fulfilment. To the proletariat nothing was more important than highlighting the excruciating pain and suffering, fun and frolics. Shaw for the first time used the dramatic art as a means of propaganda giving a new momentum to the usage of art myth and creativity. Art was used by Shaw as a new weapon for highlighting his philosophy and propaganda. As Shaw was a great realist, he brought art out of the shackles of idealism, romance and Utopia. He added a new meaning to art perception and creativity. Without the realistic exposition of the society, art for Shaw was of no use. Shaw thus brought his dramatic art to a new scale of height. Marx and Engels on the one hand made a new line of demarcation between 'haves and have-nots' gave a new socialistic outlook by virtue of which art and morality was given a new tone and tenor. Varied nuances of art thus were judged not by the nuances of morality but by a new taste of reading; a new rule of law for 'elucidation' and correction of taste was brought into vogue. Shaw popularized propaganda making art a rhetorical device, a vehicle to bring into focus all those social evils that played havoc with man and his environs. Matthew Arnold was no less involved in drawing a line of demarcation between culture and anarchy. For him culture is the main foothold on which all human aspirations rest.

A new change in style and stylistics in the rhetorical devices employed by Eliot is yet another marked departure from the traditional stock of phraseology. A new awakening infused into the colloquial language of the working classes set a new tone and tenor to the modern verse. As Eliot is averse to romanticism, he pronounced himself to be a classicist, he was baptized by the Anglican Church. In 'Prufrock and Other Observations' (1917) Eliot applies a colloquial language and a phraseology for a better communication. In Eliot's "The Love Song of J. Alfred Prufrock", "let us go then, you and I; when the evening is out against the sky" is symbolically indicative of the deep-seated ideas into the inner psyche of the modern man who measures his self in terms of trivialities of day-to-day transaction of the modern living. There is clearly a deep impact of Freud upon the colloquial language employed by Eliot. The language and the rhetorical devices in his poetry thus gave a new turf of writing poetry which was new to the contemporary society. Eliot drew impetus from Laforgue to realistically produce a language of communication to man living in the metropolis. In *The Wasteland*, the Colloquial language used by Eliot, "Hurry up please"[1] is supposed to be a part of service rendered in the pubs and restaurants. With the rise of the working classes a marked change was seen in the values of the new living modern culture. The impact of Karl Marx made deep inroads into the inner and Psychic behavior of the new emerging working lower middle classes. There was an upward rise of magazines and journals meant for catering to their new inbuilt psychic behavior. As such popular journals came into prominence with a greater frequency to give feedback to the emerging working classes keeping in view of the new growing consciousness they had from within. A new kind of journal came into vogue for catering to the taste, preference and attitude of the emerging working classes. W.H. Auden and Stephen Spender were the poets of the thirties. Having stridden their belief in the left orthodoxy, they employed a new language on a new turf of poetry, George Orwell employed a language of double speak to evade the cult of totalitarianism. In his remarkable essay "Inside the Whale" Orwell points out at the language of hypocrisy practised by the intellectuals. In "The Age of Anxiety", Auden ardently shows deep sympathy with the suffering meted out to lower middle classes having a shift from his stance given in his early poetry. D.H. Lawrence shows his commitment to the purity of art. In his "Art and Morality," the ethics of poetry and purity of art have been emphasized for bringing poetry much closer to man and nature. Lawrence laments at the declining spiritual and moral values operating in the industrial and commercialized society. For him the balance between art and morality was needed to prevent the negative impact of the colossal growth of intellect. Lawrence thus employed a new meaning; a new poetic dictum to give expression to the primitive emotion. Lawrence is no pessimist. He firmly believes that senses too can be spiritualized by following the cult of blood intimacy. In *Sons and Lovers* the new sensibility emerging into the post-industrial society on the psycho-analytical plane, points out at the new identity of the new emerging classes. Both Shaw and Eliot realistically emphasize the need to bring art out of the shackles of romantic sensibility. Art to Eliot is supposed to be seen in consonance with the collective consciousness created by tradition, myth, philosophy and culture. In his essay "Notes Towards the Definition of Culture", Eliot sincerely argued for making culture a vehicle, a medium for elucidation of work of art and correction of taste. Culture, for Eliot, is a condition for creating perception, refinement and taste. Culture, says Eliot, can be made a yardstick of corrective measure to keep the purity of art intact. Christopher Caudwell gave a new yardstick of perception to probe and see art from the socialistic angle.

Art is the soul of culture. A sense of belonging, says Eliot, is essential for the growth of finer perception and receptivity. Sampson points out at the condition for which or against which art and creativity need to be probed and examined. In his essay, "What is Classic?" (1945), Eliot stresses the follow up of the classical principles for the promotion of right kind of culture that could be an added dimension to art and perceptivity. It is however significant to add that culture is part and parcel of the 'tradition' Eliot talks of. In *After Strange Gods* (1914), tradition has been described as "rather a way of feeling and action which characterizes a group throughout generations" as such, tradition, says Eliot, involves all those habits and customs prevailing in the society we live in. Professor Salinger while reviewing Eliot's poetry writes that he not only exposes the currents and cross-currents of his age; he was "at the same time perplexed by the problem of discontinuity in culture and belief".[2]

There can be no art, says Eliot, without the implicit culture and traditions. They could be, says he, a real fulcrum for moving the spur of art. For Eliot both culture and tradition are the two ingredients that give a real condition for the growth of art, religion, myth and philosophy. While studying the restoration drama, Eliot becomes critical of the decadent culture, which was abundant with intrigue, hypocrisy and raillery. Similarly, Eliot criticizes the decadent culture of the

Jacobean age. Eliot finds too much decadence, pessimism and violence which was prevalent during the Jacobean age. Matthew Arnold defines criticism as a disinterested endeavour to hear and propagate that is best known in the world. Arnold gave topmost priority to culture for promotion of poetry. It is in this sense he interprets the meaning of morality. But Eliot was critical of Matthew Arnold for his elevating culture to the extent of religion. There are many scholars who single-handedly interpret Eliot's concept of art and creativity in the light of history, myth and tradition. To rely merely on tradition while interpreting Eliot's theory of art would be an incomplete study of the critic Eliot is. George Sampson rightly points out at the role of culture in dealing with the problem of moral hierarchy. With the rapid growth of science, commerce and industry, there has been radical shift in the thought patterns particularly in between the two World Wars. Assimilation of cultures and identities gave rise to ethnological confusion as such it can logically be said that Eliot' poetry is more or less a direct repercussion of the varied assimilation of cultures, perspectives and identities that provided him the basic raw material and infrastructure for his hearth of poetry. His major poems like "The Wasteland", "The Hollow Men" and "Gerontion" are therefore essentially an outcome of the decay of culture. Eliot is equally influenced by Arnold's disinterestedness. As such Eliot emphasizes the role of tradition in shaping up every existing generation. Arnold on the other hand projects his own canons of criticism based on religion and morality. Arnold defines criticism as a disinterested endeavour to hear and propagate that is best known in the world. The first principle of criticism, Arnold formulates, is disinterestedness which can be attained by keeping oneself aloof what he attributes to practical view of things. In Eliot's point of view, culture provides the basis on which art and literature need to be interpreted and understood. It can however be said that Eliot's decision to be naturalized as a British subject and to be Anglicized by the Anglican church, was part of his quest of the spiritual anchorage that could give sustenance to his foothold. His early poetry, on the one hand, is reminiscent of Boston. In "The Love Song of J. Alfred

Prufrock" and other poems the characters he creates are ironically oblivious of their ethos, milieu; root and cultural heritage, can be seen talking of Michelangelo without being conscious of its meaning. His later poetry is reminiscent of Mississippi River and the Dry Salvages.

Matthew Arnold's concept of culture is based on classical principles of criticism. In his "Essays on Criticism", Arnold defines the final nuances of criticism. His love of self-culture and lucidity of self-study are some of the finer aspects that project Arnold an apostle of classical principles of criticism. What is striking is that Arnold interpreted literature in terms of moral values. For him, art should be made intermingled with morality. Arnold ardently says that without poetry science would remain incomplete. Poetry, says Matthew Arnold, has the same relevance as it had for Wordsworth: "poetry is the breath and spirit of all knowledge". Arnold on the other hand says that poetry is the criticism of life. In his opinion, the greatness of a poet lies inherent in the applicability of ideas to life. It provides the basic infrastructure of thought patterns enabling us to know how to live in culturally dismantling society. Arnold significantly says that poetry of revolt against moral ideas is poetry of revolt against life. In Arnold's opinion, poetry of indifference towards moral ideas is poetry of indifference towards life. Poetry, says Matthew Arnold, is a criticism of life. As such poetry emanating from criticism of life needs to be seen in terms of the laws of poetry and truth. E.M. Forster in *Aspects of Novel* puts emphasis on symphony, rhythm and pattern much needed in a work of art. According to Matthew Arnold, the function of poetry is twofold. Firstly, it displays its function by natural faculty of expression. Secondly, it applies moral profundity in its applicability of art. Arnold's theory of criticism is principally based upon morality and role of culture. Arnold was earnestly, interested in bringing cultural values back to England and he wanted to see that all poetry should be a criticism of life. Secondly, Arnold opines that excellent objects of poetry are human actions having an inherent entrant to differentiate between moral and immoral. Arnold had no interest in the machine culture. Thirdly, Arnold says that subject is more important that action. Eliot was really influenced by Arnold's classicism. This is what Eliot signifies the role of tradition in shaping up every existing generation. In his essay *Criticism and the Reading Public*, Andor Gomme, goes on to pinpoint the cultural upheaval from mass literacy and from the enormous exercise of power. The growth of mass media, says he, too plays a crucial rule inculcated "by an apparently final decay and disintegration of traditional sanctions of belief and behavior".[3] Gomme further writes "we are at a stage in civilization which demands more and more consciousness, when the individual cannot be left to be formed by the environment but must be trained to discriminate and resist". Thus, a harmonious culture with more than individual judgment can be created in society by virtue of standards of intelligence; reason and correction of taste. An elucidation of work and correction of taste, as such, can be made possible only when high standards of intelligence and taste are allowed to exist. Gomme further writes, "failure to maintain a critical spirit means a decay in the very processes of thought and feeling."[4]

Eliot was born in America and later migrated to Britain. He studied many languages while he was reading in America. As such it is but natural that assimilation of cultures emerging there of America, England and Old India can explicitly and implicitly be seen in his poetry. Many references, allusions and symbols interwoven into his texture of poetry basically point out that Eliot was very much interested in promoting a cross-cultural understanding. Eliot's wide reading and his coming across diverse cultures and perspectives enabled him to form a cross-cultural perspective. In "The Wasteland", Eliot employs references from the Upanishad and Sanskrit. His usage of "Datta, Dayadhavam and Damyata" give; sympathies and control, have been borrowed from Sanskrit and Indian mythology. His poetic pronouncements, "Datta, Dayadhavam, Damyata", show how Eliot's wide range of reading and public perception help buildup a new intra-cultural world order for a better understanding and communication in the modern world. In "Four Quartets", Eliot thus interweaves images from the

Indian mythology creating hope for redemption and reconciliation. Impact of Ezra Pound was another major influence made upon the mind and art of T.S. Eliot, the critic and poet. It can however be realized that Pound was essentially instrumental in making Eliot formulate his theory of objective co-relative. As Eliot was averse to romanticism and to Middleton Murry's inner voice, the subjective cult of poetry. He was critical of Wordsworth's overflow of powerful feelings. In "Tradition and the Individual Talent", Eliot ardently talks of creating objective poetry emphasizing that the larger is the degree of impersonality, the larger would be the degree of perfection in a work of art. It was Ezra Pound who was instrumental in creating in Eliot an awareness to formulate his theory of objective co-relative. Poetry for Pound is something like inspired mathematics. Eliot on the one hand argues for creating objectivity and impersonality whereas Pound argues for "human equation replete with precision, simplicity and accuracy".

It can thus logically be argued that criticism is a vehicle of bringing up reformation, conception for elucidation of work of art and for correction of taste. In "Four Quartets", the impact of the Indian mythology can be felt. Unlike Freud, Jung interprets dreams and considers them as a direct outcome of the visualization of the inexpressible inner psychic process. The dreams envisioned by man says Jung, gives a sense of wholeness of personality. Their meaning and significance can be realized and comprehended in the forms of 'Mandala', a word taken from Sanskrit which stands for a circle, with a centre divided into four equal parts. What is striking is that 'Mandala' has been regarded as the oldest symbol of wholeness which remains operative in some form or other in almost all cultures. In the western classical music, a quartet is a written piece meant for four stringed instruments. It is further divided into four movements. Each movement is linked up with the scheme of analogy and contrast developed chronologically in a highly complex way and then is reviewed by varying moods of reconciliation. Jung thus points out at the 'four-ness' while the Mandal dreams are indicative of the inexplicable irritants lying inherent in the receptacle of the unconsciousness which in some way or other get evocative and find a way out through the complex symbols and illusions. In "Burnt Norton", the temporary has been contrasted with eternal. Eliot symbolically says that time-present would go on to be futile unless one experiences the timeless. Taking into account their value and eternity. Ezra Pound in identical way allows the symbols and images to get altered, changed and assimilated unless they ultimately grow into some shape, meaning and form. Pound regards these moments as magical moments in which the images, symbols and allusions turn into magical moments in his hearth of poetry. The present without the past, says Eliot, cannot have significance unless it co-exists with tradition. In "Burnt Norton" Eliot gives rather a more vivid picture of the cyclical order of time and space in which past and future get intermingled with the present—emerges the shape of the cyclical order of time through which man can have mystical power to distinguish between the flux and the eternal. The second section which is entitled as 'East Coker' is reminiscent of "Ash Wednesday" in which the protagonist who makes up his mind not to get entangled in the mundane and worldly activities with a realization that all humanistic progress and the colossal growth of science emanating thereof, end up with a big fuss. In "East Coker" the protagonist realizes the futility and insignificance of the temporal and earthly realities—compels him to realize: 'in my end is my beginning'. Similarly, in "The Love Song of J. Alfred Prufrock", Eliot employs a series of images which are suggestive of the amalgamation of varied cultures and societies. Eliot writes "let us go then you and I/ when the evening is spread out against the sky/ like a patient etherized on the table"—is symbolically suggestive of the two Eliots in the complex and multi-faceted modern life. The First World War emerged with its new sinister designs which made man caught up in a dilemma-like situation having no spiritual anchorage to define his stance of life. He is culturally degenerated to find himself rather reticent from within. He is caught up in a dilemma having no courage to open up his mind coming up with a certain purpose and goal. 'There will be time to murder and create.' He is no 'Prince of

Hamlet' rather he is 'polite, cautions and meticulous' before making the proposal of love. Love in Eliot's domain of poetry, has thus lost its sanctity. It is no more sacred in its applicability. It no more retains Keatsean sensuousness and spiritual fervour. In the "The Fire Sermon", Eliot laments at the loss of innocence and spirituality. The Thames is no more holy. The notion of cultural integrity of the modern civilization is no more intact in his poem, "The Wasteland". The modern civilization on account of the realistic cult of society in which the human endeavor is realized only in terms of the colossal growth of intellect and of the collocation of atoms, hardly addresses man's aesthetic sensibility. I.A. Richards on the other hand reiterates the interplay of impulses and the instinctual patterns of life which seek participation in every instance of human life man puts up in the postmodern society. From this standpoint, Eliot's protagonist goes on to remain a prisoner of the realistic illusive society. He goes on to live a life of bondage as the cultivation of the colossal growth of science hardly gives him any outlet to get liberation from the life of bondage in a society which realizes and contemplates its liberation in the realistic cult of society. The dominant element employed in the imagery of "Burnt Norton" on the one hand is air. In "East Coker", the dominant element is Earth. Man, says Eliot, cannot afford to live in a fragmentary life; the life should be lived and rejoiced in every moment, not in the memory of isolated moments of intensity. Jung's interpretation of 'mandal' dreams and drawings thus presents a sense of organic unity and whole-ness, can be seen as a co-relative of Eliot's "Four Quartets" in which images, symbols and pictures lying deep-seated in the inner recess of the receptacles of the human mind, find expression. The impressions associated with the "Four Quartets", are suggestive of the basic fact that all the humanistic and evolutionary progresses realized in the scientific paradise, take man to nothing but despair, disillusionment, disgust and illusion in the real and external world. In "Four Quartets", Eliot makes use of impressions; symbols get culminated into four movements. Each movement shown at a different platter draws a line of demarcation between the ethereal, the transitory and the eternal. Eliot's later poetry has a marked departure from his early poetry. In Prufrock and other observations (1917), the loss of faith and the spiritual sterility and cultural degeneration emanating thereof, has been shown on the personal plane. In his later poetry his perception becomes more poignant after he realistically sees man on the point of no return. His "Four Quartets" thus is a by product of Eliot's perception of the ultimate reality. Thus, it is the humanistic milestones achieved so far; says Eliot, bring man to the brink of spiritual decline and cultural degeneration. In "Burnt Norton", hence the idea of linking up the present with the past and future has been argued with all sincerity and tenderness. Living an epicurean life is not an answer to the human existence, the dictum that 'ripeness is all'.

In Dry Salvages many a references from the *Bhagvad Gita* have been made interwoven into the texture of Eliot's "Four Quartets". The exhortation made by Krishna to Arjuna in the *Bhagvad Gita* implies the philosophy of the disinterested action of performing one's duty without bearing the thought of any reward or action Eliot thus borrows and reiterates the basic fact of doing one's duty to the self irrespective of the fruit of labour. Eliot thus in an identical way believes in the dynamism of the dictum that work is worship. It is imperative to think, says Eliot, in terms of love's labour lost; whereas W.B. Yeats in his poem "Among School Children", art cannot be created by burning midnight oil rather artistic creativity is neither tree, nor bole, nor the trunk, it is the sum total of the tree. It would be inapt, says Yeats, to separate the dance from the dancer. Eliot thus concentrates on the present. In other words, Eliot talks of linking up both the past and the future with the present. The way up the way down, the way forward and the way backward are identical to one another. It would be a great folly to hold the belief that the time is the healer of wounds. Man cannot afford to be entrapped by appearance and illusive reality. Similarly, the impact of Indian scriptures can be seen in Somerset Maugham's novel *The Razor's Edge*. The milestone of achieving salvation, says Maugham, is not easy. The road to achieving salvation, says Somerset Maugham, is something similar to walking tiptoe on to the razor's edge. In "The Wasteland" man, says Eliot, has been shown running in a blind alley in the pursuit of happiness, which ultimately emerges to him as illusive. In Eliot's domain of poetry, the colossal growth of intellect, leads man to the illusiveness inherent in the real world. Flaubert, on the other hand, unlike Eliot takes into account the inertia of the self for the complete understanding of man and his environs. 'Fire' in Eliot's "The Wasteland", functions as a purificatory agent for cultivating purity and redemption in man. 'Fire' is thus a cathartic agent which is powerful enough to bring man back from his song of experience to the song of innocence. George Orwell, in his essay, Yogi and the commissar, intends to establish a balance between the body and soul; flesh and spirit. The greatness of Dante's *The Divine Comedy* lies in its propensity of addressing and accommodating varied cultures in the mainstream. The multiplicity of cultures can be seen falling with all their variety and diversity—is the real hallmark of Dante's concept of culture.

The American verse is based on its sense of urgency. It can be regarded as a register of his most independent minds; sensitive to the typicality of the American cultures embedded to its texture. William Cullen Byrant finds art consolatory enough to celebrate the spirit of freedom. For him nature is a mainspring giving him inspiration to define his spirit of independence. 'Freedom' and vivacity were the two words that gave impetus to the American poetry. Whitman drew inspiration from Emerson's quest of freedom who candidly added variety to American culture. For W.H. Auden poetry is a vehicle of propagating the left orthodoxy. In "The Age of Anxiety", his confession of guilt conscious feelings and frustration has been evoked. In this poem, Auden ardently employs vocabulary enthused with the spirit of liberality. Wilfred Owen, Auden, Spender and Macneice had shown their proclivity to the left orthodoxy. Unlike Pater and Oscar Wilde, Auden was of the view that poetry could make nothing happen. Williams neither agrees with Ezra Pound nor with T.S. Eliot probing the American culture in his own way. To

Williams; Eliot's "The Wasteland" was a great catastrophe for American letters because it interrupted the rediscovery of the primary impetus, the elementary principle of all art, in local conditions.[5] Apart form Pound and Eliot, Williams does not waver in between the two, he rather evolves a new method that could accommodate all those dreams Americans had. The rhythm of speech employed by Williams could nowhere be seen in the poetry of Pound and Eliot. Richard Ellmann writes: "Eliot and Pound were two myth-conscious and philosophical as well as too International...".[6] Williams on the other hand celebrates a sense of immediacy. For him the Americans should adopt only that pattern of life based upon the "scrutiny of the senses".[7]

Pound was a rebel. He did not approve of many of the ingredients of the American culture which he did not agree to. He went on remaining American in letter and spirit in spite of all his disagreement with the American ethics up to a certain degree. Getting himself detached from the poetic process, he allows the dismantling and disorganizing images and symbols in order to let them melt and amalgamate in a shape what else they could be in. Pound thus succeeds in creating harmony, beauty and pattern from hierarchy of the breaking, splitting and disorganizing images. George Sampson draws a relation between culture and literature. He basically points out at the condition of culture taking consideration of which literature need to be examined and looked into. Many a scholars of Eliot have at large emphasized the role of tradition and role of history to create an objective picture of society. But at the same time, it would be impertinent to ignore the role of 'culture' in shaping up literature and society. Hence, the impact of culture, says T.S. Eliot, is likely to affect the direction of literature. Sampson brings into focus some of the dangers inherent in popular high brow culture and their social values. As such Eliot being conscious of those dangers lying inherent in the high brow culture, in his essay, *The Use of Poetry and the Use of Criticism*, reiterates the need of 'readjustment'. Chaos and hierarchy of the images emanating out of the poetic process, says Pound are intermediary. Pound begins his poetic creativity by letting them sublimate and turn into whatsoever form and shape they carve out whereas Eliot gives a full stop to the 'broken images' in his private workshop of poetry. Eliot unlike Pound reassimilates those broken images prevailing in the real world in the Christian framework. The distorted and 'broken images' in Eliot's parameter of poetry cannot be set right unless they are brought back to their original shape, form and color. Eliot on the one hand gives a full stop to the broken images as they have been projected in the image they are. Pound on the other hand begins his poetic creativity from the dismantling and disorganizing images. He allows all those crumbling, splitting and distorting images unless they achieve a new form out of their dismantling process in his hearth of poetry. At the same time he says that sound, rhythm and color play an important role in the fragmentation itself.

It was Remy de Gourmont from whom Eliot learnt the necessity of the cultural tradition having the whole Europe changed upon. Pound was really influenced by Roden's belief that our perception of purity lies associated with the ideas of 'elucidation' and 'easy power of emotion'. On the other hand, Eliot's understanding and enjoyment are complimentary to each other. His concept of understanding and enjoyment is part of refinement of culture and heritage. The business of the poet, says Eliot, is not to find new emotions but to get them streamlined well in the involvement of the historical facts whereas Pound writes: it is the poet's business to seek correspondence, exactitude and accuracy in terms of human equation.

Sylvia Plath like Kamla Das and Emily Dickinson carries out their conviction of perception and looking at things like the way they aspire for. The poets of the thirties like Auden and Spender look at the capitalistic world with anger. The feminists like Virginia Woolf, Sylvia Plath and Kamla Das were of the view that life has to be seen with all its iota of bitterness and cruelty thrown upon the weaker sex. The feministic art with all its portrayal of the feministic vision is yet another trend setter of the global perspective. With the emergence of the cross-cultural perspective and assimilation of varied identities, a new culture has arrived on the cross-cultural scenario. As to the feministic writing brings into focus all those aspirations of the women living in the metropolis either it is art, sex and marriage; women's aspiration of the life she lives, as such has to be taken into account while identifying the post-modern society. The feminist writers look at the post-modern society with their own vision. While analyzing the dynamics of history, culture and tradition they make the things upside down. They rather upturn the appropriateness of the world saying that the writers do not write rather it is the consciousness which writes in the framework of the receptacles of the human mind. A cross-cultural perspective is a trend setter for a better insight into the post-modern society. In this context, T.S. Eliot is an apostle of the global perspective. He applies dynamics of his classical principles for setting right the ethnological confusion of the post-war Europe. Eliot, therefore, says that man without his sense of belonging and his need of spiritual anchorage, is bound to be restless. All his literary expressions either it is poetry, drama or even literary criticism will be in disarray unless he suspends disbelief in spiritual anchorage. Every genre of art he has produced thus moves round the significance of culture, identity and the need of spiritual anchorage. In his poem, "Ash Wednesday", Eliot cultivates hope, faith and affirmation of belief in myth, religion and philosophy. As such Eliot was critical of Matthew Arnold for his elevating culture to religion. No artist, says Eliot, is relevant unless he co-relates his work of art with tradition, history; myth and religion. It was this basic reason by virtue of which he advocates for making art play a subsidiary role. Art to Eliot is a mechanism or an instrument which he classically argues for maintaining the cultural standard. But the new critics like I.A. Richards, William Empson and F.R. Leavis talk of taking art in the wider perspective. In his *Principles of Literally Criticism*, I.A. Richards ardently reiterates that style is the man; the subjective emotion inherent in the self provides impetus for the artist to go for the creative process. W.B. Yeats in his master piece poem, "The Second Comings" prophesies the emergence of a new cult of violence and savagery. Eliot perceives the cult of multi-culturalism that could threaten and imbalance the spur of tradition and individual talent. F.R. Leavis goes one step ahead saying that only that dimension of tradition needs to be assimilated with existing order which is relevant and worth producing. Keeping in view of the inner cleavage hidden into the mindset of multiculturalism, he argues for developing a new global understanding which could keep society intact both culturally and spiritually. In "The Wasteland", love has lost its sanctity and its spiritual luster; the luster which was seen in Chaucer's *The Canterbury Tales*, whereas love in Eliot's "The Wasteland", has been dealt with ironically. In the modern world, says Eliot, man has been shown hankering after the realistic scientific paradise which is devoid of divine love. "The Wasteland", says Eliot, is no more sacred; 'April is the cruellest' where all hope of redemption and spiritual awakening no more exists. Therefore, the alienation and spiritual emptiness realistically explored, says Eliot, is a by product of colossal growth of assimilating cultures and identities. What Nehru aspired for was to realize various integrals of cultures come up in complete harmony so that they could fall into the homogenous and larger civilization for him is a sum total of all the integrals of cultures. For Nehru civilization becomes operative only after all the integrals of the composite cultures are not in disarray but in complete harmony. Civilization for him is a sum of total of all the integrals of culture existing in the Indian society. For Eliot culture is a yardstick to prevent the society from cultural degeneration and ethnological confusion. Eliot like Shaw and Spender is concerned with the realistic exposition of society. He saw redemption and real growth of human life in the realistic cult of society whereas I.A. Richards on the other hand reiterates the need of concentrating on the inertia of the self so that man could be part of the larger understanding. For Eliot knowledge, accumulated in the real world, leads to decay of culture, milieu and heritage.

Assertion of identity for Eliot is the last resort through which the possibility of re-integration of cultures and identities can be made possible. In "Ash Wednesday", Eliot succeeded in cultivating faith by virtue of realizing assertion of identity.

"The Wasteland", says I.A. Richards, is music of ideas. The spiral movement of the ideas inherent in "The Wasteland" symbolically points out at the various phases of the modern evolutionary life man has passed through. Eliot soon realized the emergence of the culturally assimilated society during his early life. He soon became conscious of the value of human life in the American society. The American society he saw was getting assimilated into a fragile society in which various cultures and identities were likely to be spiritually spilt up. It was this background by virtue of which Eliot had no option but to escape to the British Isle. Yeats in an identical way in his Byzantium poems, does not identify himself with the contemporary society in which redemption was seen in escaping to the holy city Byzantium where the holy sages moving in the cyclical order could purge him. In "Ash Wednesday" Eliot longs for his spiritual re-integration by not again turning to the realistic and illusive life. In "The Burial of the Dead" Eliot brings into focus the vanished romantic world of the Austro Hungarian life before 1940 which Eliot thinks led man to the ethnological confusion of the post-war Europe. As such the spiritually disorganized life Eliot realistically perceives is nothing but a 'heap of broken images'. 'London' has been regarded as an unreal city. It is worth pointing out that legend of the grail the re-integration, and the myth presented by Jessie Weston's *From Ritual to Romance.*[2] She mythologically shows the possibility of man's redemption by performing the rituals of the myth. Eliot had himself acknowledged his indebtedness to her, is indicative of his belief in the spiritual regeneration. What is ironical is that in Eliot's poetry cultural and spiritual redemption can be made possible by performing rituals. Madam Sosostris is culturally degenerated; Tiresius is blind and impotent.

Eliot's elaboration of the cultural outlook does not limit itself to the mere Western ideology but at the same time he draws impetus from the Indian mythology. In "The Wasteland", many references and allusions from the Indian mythology help him build up his global and cross-cultural understanding. In the "Fire Sermon", Eliot brings to life

Buddha's preaching against the fire of lust, anger, and envy against the seven deadly sins. His references to Buddha's teachings, bear resemblance to those preached by St. Augustine. In "What the Thunder Said" allusions from the Indian mythology have been employed to reinforce the philosophy and teachings taken from the Upanishad in which 'thunder', 'the Lord of Creation' evokes, the dictum—give, sympathize and control.

A cross-cultural perspective is a postmodern phenomenon. The growth of science and technology and the pace with which urbanization has spread all over the world contributed to the cross-cultural perspective with a new global outlook. From Goldsmith's "Deserted Village" to the steep rise in the pace of urbanization, are some of the reasons of the growth of the cross-cultural perspective. It basically gives rise to the phenomenal experiences like clash-culture and culture shock in the post-colonial society. Multiculturalism is another dimension of the cross-cultural vision in which the varied cultures, races, milieu and perspectives get inter-related. As a result an intra-cultural outlook has emerged on the socio-cultural horizon. It was E.M. Forster who had through his various novels and writings had addressed the issue of multiculturalism. The problem which he faced was that people of various races and milieu were at cross in a multicultural post-colonial world. Keeping in view of the multicultural fabric of the native-society, he was optimistic of his belief in personal relationship. Forster was of the view that man with his diverse cultural, racial and religious identities, can raise himself above his racial, parochial roots and backgrounds by celebrating the bond of personal relationship. Tagore too talks of creating a society where there would be no more cultural, racial and religious discord. In his remarkable poem, where the mind is without fear, he dreams of a decent society devoid of the cultural discord. What is a striking is that Forster, in his elaboration of the socio-cultural perspective, his concept of personal relationship alone could enable man to come up the tentacles of the cultural and racial discord irrespective of whatever be the form of discord might prevail in the society.

Hence, keeping in view of the postmodern phenomena like cross-cultural perspective, multiculturalism and assimilation of identities, it would be pertinent to say that Eliot's poetry becomes more relevant with the growth of the global and the cross-cultural perspective. Right in the beginning of Eliot's critical essays, he has emphasized how the role of 'culture' has gathered momentum in the postmodern world.

Problem of identity is one of the keynotes of poetry written after Eliot. Eliot was apprehensive of the dangers emanating from the varied assimilating identities. It could push man into cultural confusion and embarrassment. There is an implied need to evoke an awareness to create a power of faculty of reasoning in man enabling him to keep himself at par with the cultural norms and standards. It was the psychic fear in the poet that prompted him to find a way out to the cultural aberration caused by the assimilation of various identities, attitudes and milieu. Keeping in view of the jumbling and amalgamating perspectives, Eliot puts emphasis on employing corrective measures by virtue of linking up tradition with the existing order. In his plays like *The Murder in Cathedral*, *The Family Reunion* and *The Cocktail Party*, Eliot through his dramatic personae reiterates the cultivation of faith. The dramatic personae Eliot creates have been portrayed steeped in the 'real' life. The world they find themselves embroiled therein gives them no sense of belonging; crickets no relief. In *The Cocktail Party*, Eliot looks bewildered at the clash and intermingling of varied identities and perspectives. It can however be said that he presents a gloomy and pessimistic picture of the life in which man finds himself caught up in a great dilemma on account of the emergence of the assimilating cultures, races, perspectives and above all the new economic order in the aftermath of the colossal growth of the scientific paradise. Fear in Yeats' poetry also explains the fear prevailing in the inner psyche of the modern society. Yeats was pre-occupied with the feeling of otherness that envelopes his whole being. As such his ethics and aesthetics, the parameter of looking into the otherness of the outside world moves around the poet Yeats was. There are numerous striking similarities and differences between Eliot and Yeats. Like Eliot, Yeats too was well aware of the intricacies emerging on account of the influx of the varied cultures, races and multitude of new perspectives that could perplex him. It was this fear that compelled him to live confined into the ivory tower. Both Eliot and Yeats were apprehensive of the new emerging cult of violence and savagery. Both found themselves threatened by the alien surroundings. The only poetic formula Eliot could cook up was his keeping maintenance of the cultural standards which, to him alone could restrain the pace of the process of assimilation of the multitude of cultures and identities. The socialistic revolution as seen by Eliot was a hoax; a means to perplex that could make man entwined into the knots of the problem of identity. Keeping in view of emerging a new alien culture and society, Yeats, too in his early poetry keeps himself confined into the tranquility of the ivory tower where the menacingly emerging alien cultures and identities could no longer threaten his self, the self which compelled him to live at par with the Irish and Celtic cultures. Fear of the loss of identity was no less agonizing to the poets of the thirties who had proclivity to the left orthodoxy. The twin orthodoxies, the socialistic and the capitalistic patterns of society, had lots of reasons of having hostility to each other. The man-made concept of the exploiter and the exploited; 'haves' and 'have-nots' gave rise to a new solidarity. The poets of the thirties sharing anguish with each other made a new group to counter-balance their impact on the capitalistic West. W.H. Auden and Stephen Spender are the two significant poets of the thirties who showed their tilt to the left orthodoxy extending compassion for and solidarity with those who happened to be economically thrown to the periphery. The capitalistic West looked 'stranger' to the poets of the thirties who showed great compassion and solidarity for the economically marginalized. As such a new world economic order was to emerge and reshape the things to come up. Christopher Caudwell gave a new shape to the art of criticism. For him art has to be seen in terms of the popular aspirations of the people at large. Eliot was averse to the 'knowledge' that gave rise to the 'real' world where man's pursuit of happiness is limited to the rationalistic approach to life. Arthur Miller and Earnest Hemingway comment on the way the Americans rejoice success. Success to the postmodern society is ironically is the cornerstone of human aspirations. Nothing less than success can be made writ large and worth accepting to the ideals of happiness.

Dissociation of sensibility is likely to happen when the society thrives on multicultural dimensions. There can be no unified sensibility where intra-cultures along with multitude of cultures and subcultures are emerging in quest of fulfilment from the physical, psychic and spiritual aspects. 'Emotions' re-collected in tranquility cannot happen where the cross-cultural society with all its postmodern trends has inundated man both culturally and spiritually. Discordant voices getting vibrant at the assimilation of the varied cultures, perspectives and identities emerge on the socio-cultural plane with New World Order making him feel alien in the cross-cultural society. It is a society, which has lost its sanctity of time, space and consciousness. As Eliot is a great realist he realistically looks at society, which has gone awkward having its feet stridden down deep into the cross-cultural setup. In Eliot's "The Wasteland", 'knowledge' has been employed with a negative and ironical connotation, 'knowledge' attained through the endless humanistic strivings has given no spiritual and ethical ground to man. Eliot's poetic expressions with all their objective co-relatives; symbols and allusions are tinged with irony. I.A. Richards on the other hand argues for opening up the third dimension by instilling the vehicle of aesthetic pleasure into a work of art. It is the aesthetic pleasure, says Richards, which makes a work of art worth reading. Human life without aesthetic pleasure is nothing but pale and lusterless. "After such knowledge, what forgiveness?", this is how Eliot realistically exposes disintegration of culture and society. Emotions recollected in tranquility cannot take place because the postmodern society along with its varied integrals of cultures, races, identities and perspectives is basically heterogeneous. Its heterogeneity is another dimension of the postmodern society. Both Eliot and Arnold are identical in their approach to bringing about cultural harmony in the society. In Arnold's opinion, it is the disintegration of culture which gives rise to anarchy. The emergence of the cross-cultural perspective made Eliot believe that the prevailing society with all its heterogeneity is moving from culture to anarchy. C.P. Snow in his remarkable and pertinent essay critically identifies "two polar groups". Snow stylistically points out at the clash of two cultures; the clash operating between 'literary intellectuals' and scientists; Snow writes:

> No, I intend something serious. I believe the intellectual life of the whole western society is increasingly being split into two polar groups.[8]

Snow is realistic enough to identify the clash of the two cultures and comes to realize how it gives rise to a new kind of cultural dischord. Snow hence supplies a saner approach to address the problem of a new kind of conflict emanating from the clash of cultures on the artistic and moral plane. Snow writes:

> Non-scientists tend to think of scientists as brash and boastful. They hear Mr. T.S. Eliot, who just for these illustrations we can take as an archetypal figure, saying about his attempts to revive verse-drama that we can hope for very little, but that he would feel content if he and his co-workers could prepare the ground for a new Kyd or a new Greene. That is the tone, restricted and constrained, with which literary intellectuals are at home: it is the subdued voice of their culture.[9]

Recreational activities relayed by mass media in many ways, make direct impact upon the collective psyche of the British culture. What needs to be seen how culture is instrumental in establishing relation in enhancing the elucidation of work and correction of taste. The larger is the degree of high culture, the larger would be refinement in the artistic perfection and creativity. Working class culture is often regarded as popular culture. Nirad C. Chaudhuri was critical of E.M. Forster for relating art, sense and sensibility to the indigenous cultures. Popular and democratic cultures are yet other off-shoots of cultures pronouncing a new kind of vision upon the common masses. Richard Hoggart, in his essay "Mass Communication in Britain" examines the relation of culture to 'class', work and education. After the industrial revolution there had been a marked change into the consciousness of the working classes; rise of new reading public, with new preferences and attitude was seen. In "Tradition and the Individual Talent", Eliot classically argues for the elucidation of work and correction of taste. In his essay, *Notes Towards the Definition of Culture*, Eliot is of the view that high culture, which is an intermingling of art and intellectual enquiries, can contribute a lot to the elucidation of art and correction of taste. F.R. Leavis goes up one step ahead by limiting the extent to which tradition should play a guiding force. Eliot himself says that every age and every generation has its own demand and preference. F.R. Leavis takes a different step. Though Leavis agrees with Eliot that elucidation and work of art is an unavoidable necessity yet at the same time Leavis both morally and logically argues that all parts of tradition may not necessarily be relevant to the existing order. As such it would be in fitness of things to limit the role of tradition by placing the "producible text"—shows how Leavis applies the moral factor in analyzing a work of art. D.H. Lawrence likewise too argues for establishing a relation between art and morality. In other words a balanced relation between art and morality should be the basis of analyzing a work of art, says D.H. Lawrence.

In "The Wasteland", Eliot explores the theme of perversion and spiritual emptiness giving the inkling of the nature of lust that makes man succumb to the cultural aberration. There is a marked difference between the approaches of Eliot and that of Pound. Eliot on the one hand, in "Death by Water", points out at the drying up of waters, which says he, have fertilized the European Civilization. The images like cactus, rock, fire and broken column symbolize man's inability to cultivate faith in the biblical life. As such the desire for spiritual awakening invokes in Eliot's "The Wasteland". In section 1, "The Burial of the Dead", the vanished romantic world of the Austo-Hungarian aristocracy existing before 1914 reminds us of the linguistic and ethnological confusion of the post-war Europe. The cultures culminated in the realistic society, says Eliot, are nothing but 'a heap of broken images'. London is an 'unreal city' wherein its inhabitants like Lil, Albert, Eugenides, the typist, and the Thames daughters dwell with all their spiritual aridity.

Allen Gingberg attempts to outconfess confession. Sylvia Plath gathers the world into her accounts of incidents of feelings. She looks at her surroundings and surveys the outside world with despair and dejection; unable to assert herself. She writes "my hours are married to shadow/ no longer do I dislike for/ scrape of a keel/ on the blank stones of the landing."[10] Her deep-seated desire for asserting herself, provides her fire and brimstone to create consciousness enough to unfold her embittered feelings. Sylvia Plath in her bid to search for her world of consciousness, writes with all her despair and melancholy.

"You didn't just toe me an inch'/ no—'nor leave me to set/ my small bald eye/ skyward again without hope, of course/ of apprehending blueness or stars".[11] George Sampson draws a relation between culture and literature. Sampson basically points out that the condition of culture underwhich or against which literature needs to be examined.[12] Eliot at length emphasizes the role of tradition and sense of history in order to create an objective picture of society. But at the same time it would be impertinent to ignore the role of 'culture' in shaping up of literature. Hence, the impact of culture, says Eliot, necessarily affects the course and direction of literature. Sampson brings into focus some of the dangers inherent in popular high culture and social values. Sampson writes: "the chief danger now being a kind of popular high brow culture based on mass publicity and social values are still sufficiently with us".[13] Eliot in his another essay, *The Use of Poetry and the Use of Criticism* reiterates the need of 'adjustment'. Prof. Salinger while making review of Eliot's poetry writes that he not only explores the currents and cross-currents of his age but at the same time Eliot was perturbed at "the problem of discontinuity in culture and belief".[14] Aldous Huxley points out at the 'power' of words clarifying how it became a vehicle of transmitting knowledge and information by the mass media. The 'imaginative literature', says Aldous Huxley, plays an important rule in influencing the consciousness of the modern generation. Huxley writes that in the present time, the cinema acts far more effectively as the opium of the people than does religion. Hence, he identifies the impact of "imaginative literature upon its readers".[15] As Eliot pronounced himself to be a classicist, he shows deep love for the classical literature. Eliot saw that the realistic cult of society was a sum total of the colossal growth of science and intellect but devoid of spirituality. Huxley like Eliot says that man has scientifically progressed making the society he lives in, turns into a scientific paradise. But ironically the scientific paradise he lives in is devoid of 'wisdom'. Thus, both Eliot and Huxley share their common belief that man's attainment of knowledge is devoid of 'wisdom'. In his significant poem, "Gerontion", Eliot ironically writes that the colossal growth of intellect hardly gives spiritual anchorage to man. "After such knowledge what forgiveness?" this is how Eliot ironically remarks at the abnormal growth of the human mind. Huxley identically writes: "And, in 'The Wasteland', Mr. Eliot uses the same metaphor".[16] Huxley also says that the people of the West do not carry with them a literature and the system of ancient wisdom; "The common ground of all the Western cultures has slipped away from under our feet".[17] C.P. Snow in his remarkable and pertinent essay critically identifies two polar groups. Snow stylistically points out at the clash of two cultures; the clash operating between "literary intellectuals and scientists". Snow writes: "No, I intend something serious I believe the intellectual life of the whole of western society is increasingly being split into two polar groups".[18]

Eliot was at the same time a critic of social and cultural aspects of life. He acquired British citizenship in 1927 which was confirmed by the Church of England. Eliot's social and cultural aspects have been widely dealt with in his essays like *Thoughts After Lambeth*, (1931) *After Strange Gods* (1934), *The Idea of a Christian Society* (1939), *Notes Towards*

Definition of Culture. Richard Ellmann, making review of Eliot's poetry, writes:

> In view of Eliot's decision to be naturalized a British subject and to be received in the Anglican church, his status as American poet may seem jeopardized.[19]

Poetry, says Yeats, is truth seen with passion. Promoting his opinion upon Pound's poetry, Yeats writes: "Probably too much attention has been paid to the technique of the cantos at the expense of its contents."[20] It is because Pound's ideas and subject matter are important in themselves that poetry is living. In Arnold's domain of poetry, on the other hand, poetry has been elevated to the status of religion. Modern man has been portrayed as an alert man. It is difficult for him to cling to one single identity. What is striking is that Eliot's poetry is the assimilation of varied perspectives, backgrounds and identities giving rise to a new form of poetry which could accommodate discordant voices and verisimilitude of identities. Hence, Stephen Spender gives anthropological definition of Eliot's "The Wasteland". In his opinion "The Wasteland" is suggestive of the prevailing modern life. It is at the same time suggestive of the inbuilt merging identities. Archetypal identities in, "The Wasteland", emerge from the larger identities. The Smyrna merchant who is identified with the Tarot one eyed merchant, is later identified with the Phoenicial sailor. The one eyed merchant, on the other hand, melts into the Phoenician sailor. In this way, the protagonist represents both sides of the proposition. Thus, Eliot employs usage of complex symbols suggesting how the diverse identities get merged into a different identity.

Much of Murry's criticism deals with his own society and education; whereas Leavis intends to concentrate on university education in English. Leavis started writing in 1930; the pamphlet on mass civilization and minority culture, itself shows his uncompromising stand on the Marxists. E.M. Forster, on the other hand, was caught up between the problem of multiculturalism and his vision of personal relationship. George Sampson studies the age of T.S. Eliot and establishes relation between criticism and culture. Sampson specifies the writers like Dickens, Joyce, Naipaul and other West Indian novelists who have contributed a lot to the emergence of a new diction, rhythm and speech through their writings. Sampson writes: "Such writers, novelists and poets alike have brought a new idiom in every sense, to literature in English language, as their calypso-singing compatriots have brought a new rhythm to popular music and their cricketers a new vitality to sport"[21] whereas Richard Ellmann, in his *The New Oxford Book* realizes the after effects of assimilation of the American and the British rhythms and speeches. Richard Ellmann writes:

> Eliot and Pound were too myth-conscious and philosophical as well as too international.[22]

Bertrand Russell like Eliot is also critical of the colossal growth of the realistic society. He realistically argues that 'knowledge is power' but at the same time, he points out at the dangers inherent in the enormous growth of 'knowledge', which could upturn the apple cart of the humanistic developments man has achieved so for. Russell writes: "Knowledge is power, but it is power for evil just as much as for good. It follows that, unless men increase in wisdom as much as in knowledge, increase of knowledge will be increase of sorrow."[23] M.K. Gandhi on the other hand does not appreciate the cult of multiplication followed by the European civilization. Gandhi in his essay, "Indian Culture and Civilization" compares the Western civilization with the Indian culture. Western civilization, says Gandhiji, is the worship of the material. He is of the view that real happiness can be cultivated in the curtailment of wants. Images recollected in tranquility thus bring him back to the ideas of the possible closed door which perhaps would have opened into a rose garden-taking him to the basic realization of affirmation of hope. In "Four Quartets", the garden is suggestive of multiplicity of ideas, images and reminiscences coming on to the consciousness of the poet. It could be suggestive of childhood, fancy, deceptive notes of fantasy; it could be an escape from the mundane world away from the world of alienation. Thus, Eliot's poetry is a melting pot of identities in which diverse identities get assimilated. Eliot's poetry pays attention to the arrival of a new cross cultural identity with all its preferential and behavioural patterns. In fact, Eliot, unlike his contemporaries, evolves a new modus operandi to explore the currents and cross currents, preference; traits and attitudes ensconced in the cross cultural identity.

NOTES

1. T.S. Eliot, *The Wasteland*, p. 56.
2. *The Pelican Guide of English Literature*, Vol. 7, edited by Boris Ford, ed. 1970, p. 335.
3. Andor Gomme, "Criticism and the Public Reading", *The Pelican Guide to English Literature*, Vol. 7, edited by Boris Ford, Penguin Books, ed. 1970, p. 351.
4. *Ibid.*, p. 353.
5. *The New Oxford Book of American Verse*, p. xvi.
6. *Ibid.*
7. *Ibid.*
8. C.P. Snow, *The Two Cultures, Aspects of English Prose*, selected and edited by K.M. Tiwary, R.C.P. Sinha, Vikas Publishing House, Pvt. Ltd., ed. 1988, p. 80.
9. *Ibid.*, pp. 80-81.
10. *The New Oxford Book of American Verse*, p. 1038.
11. *Ibid.*, p. 1051.
12. George Sampson, *The Concise Cambridge History of English Literature*, Vikas Publishing House Ltd., ed. 1975, p. 929.
13. George Sampson, *The Concise Cambridge History of English Literature*, 3rd edition, Vikas Publishing House, Pvt. Ltd., New Delhi, ed. 1975, p. 915.
14. *The Pelican Guide to English Literature*, The Modern Age, edited by Boris Ford, Vol. VII ed., p. 335.
15. *Essays of Aldous Huxley*; selected and edited by S.K. Kumar Macmillan India Limited, Madras, ed. 1988, p. 178.
16. *Ibid.*, p. 179.
17. *Ibid.*
18. C.P. Snow, *The Two Cultures, Aspects of English Prose*, selected and edited by K.M. Tiwary, R.C.P. Sinha, Vikas Publishing House Pvt. Ltd., ed. 1988, p. 80.

19. *The New Oxford Book of American Verse*; chosen and edited by Richard Ellmann, New York, Oxford University Press, ed. 1976, p. XXVVIII.
20. Ezra Pound, *Selected Prose*; Faber and Faber, Ltd., London, edited with introduction by William Cookson, ed. 1973, p. 7.
21. George Sampson, *The Concise Cambridge History of English Literature*, third ed., Vikas Publishing House, Pvt. Ltd., New Delhi, ed. 1975, p. 1934.
22. *The New Oxford Book of American Verse*, p. XIV.
23. Bertrand Russell, *The Impact of Science on Society*, Blackie & Son (India) Ltd., ed. 1969, p. 164.

7

Post Script

Eliot's place in modern poetry is different from that of his contemporaries. Like Auden and Spender, Eliot belongs to both the American and the British traditions. The intermingling of the two traditions in Eliot, solipsistically gave rise to the two Eliots, "You and I" that found expression in his early poetry. Eliot realistically saw how in the postmodern society, the process of crumbling and splitting up of personality started dismantling the American tradition. With the emergence of new realism, Robert Frost like Gold Smith laments at the diminution of the rural landscapes. Thoreau is a typical American who delineates the thought patterns much needed for the ethical growth of the human mind. Ezra Pound, in his own way, draws attention to the quintessence of the spirits of freedom claimed by the human soul. It is in this sense that Pound propounds the 'human equations' and the 'inspired mathematics' for exploring human situations with utmost accuracy.

The basic driving force behind Eliot's projection of the objective co-relative was his yearning for the extinction of personality. Poetry for Eliot hence is not the 'turning loose of emotion' but escape from emotion. He was therefore averse to the assimilation of emotion in a work of art. The objective co-relative employed by Eliot thus enables him to orchestrate the manifold discursive voices of the self. What can basically be argued is that the perception implicit in personal and subjective experiences, which go on to persist as the basic infrastructure of the vehicle of objective co-relative. As Eliot projected himself to be a classiest, it can logically be argued that he intends to carve out a balance between knowledge and immediate experience. What is striking is that if a personal experience for Eliot is a primary imagination of an artist, the objective co-relative carved out by him, is the secondary and extended metaphor of the personal and subjective emotions which he experiences in the beginning of the process of artistic creativity. Unlike I.A. Richards and Flaubert, Eliot is a realist par excellence. Hence, the personal feelings and the immediate experience which Eliot intermingles in his private workshop of poetry, principally emanates from his personal and subjective emotions. Eliot walks up all alone carrying with himself all those feelings of dejection, despair and anguish which he had himself experienced halfway there in Boston. Eliot could not have turned full circle unless he had gone across up to the British Isles. Inventing the objective co-relative for putting up those feelings of anguish, pain, despair, grief and loneliness was the need to cohere them with those feelings of dejection and pessimism with utmost objectivity. The logic behind Eliot's objective co-relative is basically to find a way out to the anguish and despair he had himself experienced while he was writing his early poetry. The individual talent to him is a sum total of all those elements of anguish, nostalgia and of the embittered feelings which had made him basically melancholic and pessimistic. His search for spiritual anchorage becomes cross-cultural in his realistic exposition of the society as depicted in "The Wasteland", "Ash Wednesday" and "Four Quartets". The tone and tenor of the images, symbols and rhetorical devices employed therein to restrain the subjective emotion, become more intense and sharp in his later poetry which ultimately act as an extended metaphor in Eliot's poetry. Eliot projects a sense of urgency to dig up the past and know where his roots actually lay. Therefore, the images, symbols and the rhetorical devices employed in his poetry cannot achieve transcendence unless the objective co-relative he builds up, is taken to be an intermingling or a medium or a vehicle of striking a balance between immediate experience and dissociation of sensibility. What Eliot symbolically endeavors is to seek various ways and means in order to evolve a mechanism; a resolution to find an alternative pinpointing myth, philosophy and religion which to him are more important than art and creativity. Art to T.S. Eliot is synonymous with the past and the historical sense. For Eliot art has to be seen in conformity with tradition and involvement of the historical fact. Yeats was an artist of a different kind. Unlike Eliot he does not talk of assimilating identities, cultures and perspectives. Instead, he prefers to live confined into the ivory tower where his self cannot be threatened by the external illusive realistic world. Orwell evolves the double speak to sustain the multiplicity of cultures and perspectives in order to survive in the real and the external world. In the Byzantium poems, Yeats yearns for escaping to the world where he is no more threatened by the external illusive realistic world. The images and symbols employed in the Byzantium poems, take him to the world beyond the mundane and the real world; it is a world, where he is supposed to be purged of all mundane realities which made him spiritually sick.

Mahatma Gandhi ardently agued for a culture, which was based upon truth and non-violence. To him attainment of knowledge would be futile and trivial if knowledge is attained only for the sake of knowledge and artificiality. Build up your character, says Mahatma Gandhi, before you attain education. As culture to Mahatma Gandhi would be meaningful unless a true seeker of knowledge and wisdom goes on to the extent of purging of his own ingrained evil is the basis for him for promotion of world culture. In his remarkable, "The Way to the Equal Distribution", Gandhi argues for a society based upon truth, non-violence and contentment. A rationalistic behavior based on truth and compassion, says Gandhi, plays a significant role in shaping up man for creating a milestone of the global culture; the capitalists have been regarded as no more than a custodian of the wealth of the poor. 'Knowledge' devoid of character and spirituality will bring nothing says he but chaos and disorder in the society. Appreciating the contribution made by Gandhi to the Indian people, Jawaharlal Nehru writes: "He made them think of political and economic issues, and every village and every bazaar hummed with argument and debate on the new idea and hopes that filled the people."[1] The role of culture on the other hand promoted by Gandhi is to make people basically conscious of the socio-economic and cultural identity, which they belong to. His revolutionary ideas of politics and society made inroads into the human psyche enabling them at the same time, to fall in line with the global cultures. Pandit Nehru further writes: "Gandhi was that leader, and he released many of the bonds that imprisoned and disabled our minds, and none of us who experienced it can ever forget that great feeling of release and exhilaration that came over the Indian people."[2]

Eliot was bewildered at the colossal growth of intellect in the realistic society. For Eliot it is the culmination of the colossal growth of science which gives rise to alienation, rootlessness and spiritual imbecility. Such culmination of the scientific paradise, says he, has brought man to the point of no return; After such knowledge what forgiveness? this is how Eliot points out at the pathetic fallacy in the attainment of 'knowledge'. Knowledge attained by virtue of the humanistic processes, says Eliot, brings nothing rather it ends is up in a fuss. What is a striking; is that Eliot applies the corrective measures in order to make varied cultures fall in line with history and tradition. Therefore, it would be in the fitness of things to say that it is not the alienation, rootlessness and spiritual imbecility rather it is his ignoring the instinctual patterns which become the root cause of his splitting up of identity. I.A. Richards studies the problem of identity with a new vision where the soul itself seeks participation in every stance of life either in a work of art or in poetry or in bringing up of culture. Serious poetry emerges, says Richards, when the overflow of emotion is allowed to be made part of a work of art.

Man while living in the Chaucerian era had real fervor and taste for romance and solitude. Love for chivalry and romance of the jungles had its own charm, color and spiritual manifestation. Love during the medieval society was not achievable without spiritual manifestation. There was real zest for visiting the places of worshiping God where man could hope for redemption. April in Chaucer's "Canterbury Tales" brought with it a spiritual awakening. The images of April and symbols associated with spiritual sickness in Eliot's "The Wasteland" have been used with an ironical meaning. There is a little hope for spiritual awakening for a man living in the 'unreal' city. Thomas Gray portrays a beautiful picturesque of the dusky evening. He employs subjective images in painting the rural landscapes in the medieval society. In Chaucer's The Canterbury Tales, man usually loved visiting places of worship whereas April, in Eliot's "The Wasteland", is the cruellest month, enkindling no spiritual warmth, ironically has been contrasted with the emergence of the new identity of man and his culture. 'Thames' is no more sacred. 'Nymphs' have departed, says Eliot, with the emergence of the cross-cultural civilization. The images like stone, fire and Cactus are symbolically suggestive of the spiritual aridity of the neo-culture which happens to stride its feet in the realistic society Eliot attributes it to a by-product of the colossal growth of science and intellect. Eliot writes: "The river bears no empty bottles, sandwich paper,..." The "Hollow Men" are culturally degenerated devoid of faith in the historical and biblical wisdom. They are, to Eliot, papers, silk handkerchiefs, card board boxes. The river bears no empty bottles, sandwitch papers/silk handkerchiefs, cardboard boxes, cigarette ends/or other testimony of summer nights. The nymphs are departed."[3] They are 'headpiece filled with straw'. Their lack of spiritual and cultural sense and sensibility does hardly have anything with itself, which could create poetry, form, pattern, symphony, meaning and direction to their day-to-day business of life. They can hardly expect any artistic creativity out of their mundane life. Their real problem, says Eliot, is how to strike a balance between thought and action. Eliot's dissociation of sensibility therefore is a direct impact of the emerging diverse cultures, dialects and vehicle of the language employed in the metropolis. Thomas Carlyle like Eliot delves deep into the currents and cross-currents of the past and present. He shows all love for the modern society and makes himself indifferent to whatever exists outside his moral philosophy. Carlyle curtails those elements of the present, which do not assimilate, with his concept of morality. G.K. Chesterton on Carlyle writes: "it is certainly better to reject that which one cannot assimilate."[4] But Eliot does not show the extent to which the existing order could be assimilated with the past. It was F.R. Leavis who gives the line and length and the extent to which the possibility of assimilation of cultures and identities could be made. V.S. Naipaul attributes it to the enigma of the human existence. Each and every riddle of human life he intends to know, the more it adds to the degree of his confusion and perplexity.

In his letter written to Harriet Monroe, Pound delineates definition of poetry in 1915. Poetry, says Pounds, "must be as well written as prose". Simplicity and meaning are the two basic elements which must be the sole prerequisite of poetry. In Pound's domain of poetry, there is no room for paraphrases and inversions. He puts aside the set phrases or rhymes which are provided for the sake of rhythm. The role of rhyme in Pound's scheme of poetry, conveys and delivers meaning. Great literature, says Pound, should always be equipped with "meaning to the utmost meaning". Pound principally puts emphasis on the method of the Chinese ideographs. Pound's ideographic method, hence, is a synchronization of the concrete poetic proposition.

The panaroma projected by Eliot's poetic canvas, presents the realistic picture of society. The images, symbols and rhetorics carry within the twilight vision of his early poetry. The poetic infrastructure which is part of his workshop of poetry, assimilates all those areas of perception concealing those emotions of despair. Thus, the need to camouflage his twilight vision, receives impetus primarily from the subjective emotions. Therefore, it would be in fitness of things to state that the symbols, allusions and vehicles of expression built up to create art of ambivalence, enabled him to project his subjective and personal experiences on the impersonal plane. Thus, scraping of reconciliatory ideas through the mechanism of the objective co-relative, projects his discursive ideas and images assimilating them into a larger identity. In Eliot's dynamics of poetry, varied identities get submerged into one ultimate identity. In "Ash Wednesday", Eliot's search for ultimate identity reflects from his discursive experiences. V.S. Naipaul undertakes journey and digs up the past. The agony of un-entwining the threads of identity basically provides him the requisite impetus to have a comparative account of both sides of the Atlantic. Naipaul ironically remains caught up into the web of the enigma of arrival. The human existence to him is nothing but a big riddle. Naipaul nowhere sees the enigma of arrival unravelled during his journey undertaken by him. He endlessly acts with ant-like business and goes on to play with the riddle of life. He rationalistically goes on to argue exploring the areas of 'darkness' he comes across. Eliot cultivates faith and affirmation of hope in his later poetry particularly in "Ash Wednesday", "Marina" and "Four Quartets". From this standpoint, it would be improper to say that Eliot was a wanderer. Both Naipaul and Eliot undertake journey from pillar to post in search of their cultural heritage. What is striking is that Eliot is no escapist as he realistically believes that the pulsating beat of the self cannot allow man to ignore the raw and unrefined aesthetic emotion. Even after he got himself shifted from America to that of the British Isles, Eliot could not harp those basic, primitive, rudimentary and subjective emotions that went on to haunt his mind and became part of his phantasmagoria. In *The Family Reunion*, Harry suffers from the illusion of committing the guilt itself shows how it menacingly goes on to be a nightmarish experience. Eliot's carrying out the objective co-relative and his usage of allusions and images is not the end of imaginations instead they symbolically with all their art and subjectivity, project Eliot's vastness of poetic imagination.

Eliot walks up all alone carrying with himself all those feelings of dejection, despair and anguish which he hid himself experiencing half way there in Boston. Eliot could not have turned full circle unless he had gone across up to the British Isles. Projecting the objective co-relative for putting up those feelings of anguish, pain, despair, grief and loneliness, was the need to cohere them with those feelings of utter dejection, pessimism with utmost objectivity. The logic behind Eliot's objective co-relative, hence is basically to find a way out to the anguish and dilemma he had himself experienced. The Individual Talent to him is a sum total of all those anguish, nostalgia and the embittered feelings which made him basically melancholic and pessimistic. His search for spiritual anchorage becomes cross-cultural in his realistic exposition of the society as depticted in "The Wasteland". The tone and tenor of the images, symbols and rhetorical devices employed to restrain the subjective emotion, become more intense and sharp in his later poetry acts as an extended metaphor.

Eliot realizes the pathetic fallacy hidden in the colossal growth of science and intellect which no longer caters to aesthetic emotion. What is ironical is that a pallor of groom, pessimism and melancholy envelops the whole being of Eliot, the poet who could envision how various perspectives and identities torment man on the existential plane. It can thus be said that the characters Eliot portrays on his poetic canvas are sad and pessimistic having no hope for their attainment of redemption. All sorts of scientific, intellectual and above all humanistic developments man has achieved so far, annihilate the human endeavour in the post-modern context. The colossal growth of science and intellect man has achieved, says Eliot, cannot achieve transcendence as it leads man to nothing but to the 'algebra of infinities'. Being beset with the diverse cultures and perspectives, man in Eliot's domain of poetry, feels the evocativeness of the inner self. The pallor of gloom goes on to cut deep into him as he finds himself dislocated from the mainstream of life. What is bewildering to Eliot is that he does not know how to tackle the problems emanating from amalgamation of identities, cultures and varied perspectives. George Orwell in *Animal Farm*, identically grapples with the problem of the mingling identities. Man is in the Orwellian World, has been shown embarrassed at the concealment of emotion. It is the vehicle of the double speak which enables to hide his stark emotion. Yeats is bewildered at the arrival of the beastly and violent culture. Eliot, on the other hand, was bewildered at tackling the problem of identity. For Eliot getting streamlined with tradition and sense of history, could alone create a sense of belonging. Nothing less than identity and spiritual anchorage would give comfort to man.

Various methods of criticism have already been applied. F.R. Leavis and Vyvor Winters have applied moral evaluation of literature. In F.R. Leavis' "The Great Tradition", great works of literature have been evaluated from the moral standpoint. Jane Austen, Joseph Conrad, and Dickens belong to Leavis' great tradition. Freud's theory of sex and psycho-analytical insight into the human psyche made a tremendous impact upon the new emerging trends of modern literary criticism. Alder on the one hand points to the concept of inferiority complex, Jung opens up a new horizon of literary criticism and perceives 'wholeness' in the collective unconsciousness. Jung finds a logical association and co-relation between "Mandela" a word taken from Sanskrit. Eliot's "Four Quartets" necessarily gives "wholeness" to a work of art. From Jung's opinion dreams are suggestive of the inbuilt thoughts, ideas and images lined up deep-seated into the collective unconscious. What is worth pointing out in Jung's concept of the collective unconscious is that the collective unconscious—is itself a greater reality. Jung's concept of the collective unconscious has been applied to literary criticism by I.A. Richards, Edmund Wilson and F.L. Lucas. They basically point out at the basic fact how psychology gives an added dimension while interpreting various forms of literature. Eliot's theory of criticism on the other hand moves round religion and philosophy. I.A. Richards in his *Practical Criticism* makes his semantic principle the basis of his theory of criticism—has been branded as New Criticism. Taking a different stand which is contrary to, Eliot's, the new critics gave a new direction to modern criticism. The new critics are of the view that both content and form are not separate from each other rather they co-exist.

Eliot was not only a critic of literature but also a critic of social and cultural aspects of human life. He acquired British citizenship in 1927 which was confirmed by the Church of England. Eliot's views on social and cultural aspects have already been widely dealt with in his works like *Thoughts*

After Lambeth (1934), *After Strange Gods* (1934), *The Idea of a Christian Society* (1939), *Notes Towards Definition of Culture* (1948). Eliot says that the larger is the degree of objectivity, the larger is the degree of perfection in a work of art. Defining the role of a perfect critic, Eliot says, business of a critic essentially has to be objective and impersonal. Ezra Pound who had exercised a great influence on Eliot, was his mentor. Pound who was well-versed with literature of Japan, Italy, France and Chinese, played a great role in arranging thoughts and contents in a chronological order. Eliot who was baffled by the intermingling of the multitude of varied identities, sought for bringing those diverse experiences to a discipline which he himself acknowledged. Pound did not create the poets but he created a situation in which for the first time there was a modern movement in poetry in which, English and American poets collaborated, knew each other's works and influenced each other. In the *Selected Essays*, Eliot criticises Arnold who regarded culture as religion. Eliot is, therefore, critical of Matthew Arnold holding him responsible for making culture subservient. He says that there is possibility of inter-relationship of religion and art but if culture is elevated to the extent of religion, says Eliot anarchy of feeling dominates religion. Many critics like Vincent Buckley and F.R. Leavis have pointed out some of the limitations of Eliot's art of poetry. Vincent Buckley in *Poetry and Morality* holds the view that Eliot regards emotion inferior to thought. He finds ambivalence and ambiguity in the treatment of emotion in the poetic process. The purpose behind evolving the objective co-relative, says Vincent Buckley is to avoid any direct emotion in his poetic process. Vyvor Winters on the other hand regards Eliot as a poet of automation. It is Eliot's primacy to thought than to feeling itself shows how he avoids the doctrine of the inner self in his making of art.

Eliot's poetry hence can be regarded as an outcome of cultural blindness. In "The Wasteland", Eliot raises his voice against the emergence of socialistic powers. Eliot opines the socialistic culture emerging on the socio-cultural scenario caters too much to the body and is hence devoid of the requisite faith much needed for the harmonious living. Eliot writes:

> What is that sound high in the air
> Murmur of maternal lamentation
> Who are those hooded hordes swarming
> Over endless plains, stumbling in cracked earth.[5]

The socialists on the other hand are of the view that culture is the basis on which rests the relevance of art. Christopher Caudwell looks at culture from the socialistic stand-point. Cultures says he, are exponents of the socialistic philosophy making art living. Eliot instead says that culture devoid of the requisite faith results in chaos and disorder. The writers who advocated for the art for art's sake, on the other hand, opine that art cannot play a subsidiary role in a work of art. Eliot in his various critical essays holds the view that art based upon the involvement of the historical sense, comes to the aid of culture. Eliot's theory of creativity is thus twofold. To Eliot both criticism and culture equally have relevance in the artistic creativity. As such he puts emphasis on the promotion of culture under which a work of art needs to be interpreted and shaped up. Art, says Pater, itself is significant. It does not need to play a subservient role in the creativity of a work of art, says he. To Eliot, criticism and culture are equally important to present a complete picture of life. For Eliot nothing is more important than involving the sense of history in the existing order. No art, says Christopher Caudwell, has relevance unless the culture of the proletariat is evoked therein a work of art. It was in this sense that the left orthodoxy argued against the bourgeois-culture. The phenomenal experiences like clash culture and culture shock gave a new twist and turn to the new emerging trends to the society. Eliot systematically brings into focus all those thought patterns in order to create a unified sensibility. Eliot is essentially a great poet of despair and pessimism. The emerging colossal growth of the realistic society devoid of the aesthetic emotion, dissociates his sensibility. The images like broken column, heap of broken images, stone and cactus hardly give an inkling of hope. All the humanistic and scientific developments taking place in the 'real' society, says Eliot, make man undergo a Kafkayesque experience. Eliot's usage of the colloquial language is thus an unavoidable necessity for realistically exposing the diverse cultures. In his later poetry what made Eliot perturbed was how to create a unified sensibility in a society in which a multitude of varied identities and cultures commingle with one another. Thus, it was his lingering need to realize the unified sensibility which made Eliot look up for the spiritual anchorage. His "Datta, Damyata and Dayadhavam"; give, sympathies and control, are derivatives taken from the Indian mythology. Eliot's poetry is thus an assimilation of both the Eastern and the Western cultures. In his poems like "Ash Wednesday", "Four Quartets" and "Marina", a new Eliot comes into being reposing requisite faith in the Anglican Church. Freud was psycho-analytically conscious of the deep inset of the cleavage inherent in the substance of the human mind. In the "Four Quartets", the cultural variables have been looked into and resolved at length in which the time past and present commingle into one. In "Marina", Eliot looks up for redemption. Redemption in Marina is made possible by renunciation of the world. Marina is restored to her old father who had believed her to be dead. The images like 'Woodthrush' and 'timbers' employed in 'Marina' evoked Eliot's renewal of hope in the 'time beyond'. Eliot writes;

> Living to live in a world of time beyond me; Let me
> Resign my life, for this life, my speech for that unspoken,
> The awakened, lips parted, the hope, the new ships.[6]

Thus, in "Marina", separation is replaced by union; pessimism by affirmation of hope. Eliot's usage of the unspoken word symbolizes his firm belief in the biblical, metaphysical and spiritual order. In "Ash Wednesday", Eliot identically relies on 'the unheard' and the 'unspoken'. In his later poetry, he no longer looks back to the materialistic world. The resilience of hope and redemption, says Eliot, can only be realized in 'the unspoken word' on the metaphysical plane. Eliot writes: "If the lost word is lost, if the spent word is spent/ if the unheard, unspoken/ Word is unspoken, unheard;/ Still is the unspoken word, the Word unheard,/ The word without a word, the Word within."[7]

Aldous Huxley realizes the power of words and how they become a vehicle of transmitting knowledge. The 'imaginative literature', says Aldous Huxley, plays a significant role in influencing the collective consciousness of the modern society. Huxley writes: "At the present time, the cinema acts far more effectively as the opium of the people than does religion".[8] Taking into account the magical effects of imaginative literature upon readers, Huxley identifies the impact of imaginative literature upon Eliot's poetry. Huxley writes: "And, in 'The Wasteland', Mr. Eliot uses the same metaphor."[9] Huxley hence draws up a line of demarcation between "Knowledge and Wisdom". Eliot is thus a great critic of the realistic cult of society. The endless growth of the humanistic progress with all its knowledge and information, says he, makes man confused and bewildered in the socio-cultural fabric of the Indian society. I.A. Richards, hence puts emphasis on creating the third space—which enables man to define his aesthetic emotion in the 'real' world. Richards reiterates that a great discrepancy takes place between the self and the outside 'real' world on account of the lack of applicability of the aesthetic emotion.

Eliot opines that the larger is the degree of objectivity and impersonality, the larger would be the degree of perfection in a work of art. Ezra Pound, on the other hand, categorically emphasizes the need of writing poetry the way the ideographs emerge in a work of art. F.R. Leavis was more Elioton than Eliot. Leavis gives a new definition of poetry which is much different from that of poetry given by Eliot. Eliot therefore relentlessly argued for assimilation of the existing of order with the pastness of the past. But unlike Eliot, Leavis limits the extent to which assimilation of diverse identities should be made. He rather interlinks poetry with morality. Leavis applies his logistics on reasoning which element of tradition is relevant to the existing order. Eliot arguably in his essay "Tradition and the Individual Talent", says that each and every generation has its own attitudes, traits and preferences.

T.S. Eliot is a by product of the international and cross-cultural perspective. He was realistically conscious enough to see that the emerging socialism and cosmopolitanism have replaced the concept of racial superiority practised during the Victorian era. Kipling believed in the White Man's burden that could have replaced the ignorance prevailing during the British Era. E.M. Forster in his novel, *A Passage to India* at length discusses various ways and means through which a common passage could be held and human relationships could exist between nations as well as between individuals. Forster thus ardently argues for creating a world where religious and cultural harmony could be made possible. In Forster's world, there is no room for hatred, prejudice and racial superiority where no one could claim or assert superiority—religious, cultural and in whatsoever form it could be, nor any nation could assert superiority in either form; religious or cultural standpoints. Likewise, Eliot too advocates that England's literary isolation should come to an end. Eliot was thus a great disciple of Ezra Pound. In Mauberley poems, Pound unfolds his concept of the world he intended to create by shaping up America in the mould of the European confederation. In Henery James 'Portrait of a Lady', the picturesque of the American model of society can be vividly seen. Elizabeth the heroine of the novel dreams of her marriage only after she sees the whole of Europe. Thus being a prototype of Henery James, Pound says that America modelled on the cast of European civilization, would have been turned into a decent society. Yeats saw the modern society languishing in the moral hierarchy. Like Ezra Pound, Eliot, hence regarded English literature as a part of European literary tradition, right from Homer onwards. Pound, on the one hand, puts emphasis on the assimilation of the American and the European cultures. Eliot, on the other hand, in the identical ways, puts emphasis on cosmopolitanism; assimilation of cultures and the study of comparative literature—which is the hallmark of his poetry.

Eliot was the creation of Ezra Pound. Pound expounded poetry in terms of ideographs. Poetry for him is no exaggeration but something like a 'good prose'. Poetry for Pound is no different from simple and good prose which could be seen manifest in the Chinese ideographs. Perhaps Eliot might have drawn inspiration from Pound for creating objectivity in his poetry. Another major influence that made a great impact upon Eliot, was Matthew Arnold. Arnold had enthusiastically wanted to create 'disinterestedness' in a work of art whereas Eliot in his various essays, puts emphasis on the need of extinction of personality and on separating art from artist.

T.S. Eliot, on the other hand dispels the charges made by Richards saying that "his psychology of poetic experience is based upon his own experience of poetry, as truly as his theory of value arises out of his psychology."[10] Clarifying his concept of poetry Eliot puts emphasis on 'reorganization'. In *The Frontiers of Criticism*, Eliot puts emphasis on understanding and enjoyment saying that both understanding and enjoyment are complementary to each other. In *The Use of Poetry and the Use of Criticism*, Eliot again draws attention to the basic fact that the element of the enjoyment adds up and enhances the area of understanding which ultimately, says he, creates original, "the original intensity".[11] Eliot attributes it to "a second stage in our understanding of poetry, when we no longer merely select or reject but organize".[12] Therefore, the implied necessity, says Eliot, is the reorganization of both the elements of understanding and enjoyment. Richards on the other hand puts emphasis on the play of verbal and classroom-interpretation of work of art whereas Eliot opines that "Education in poetry requires an organization of this experiences".[13] But Richards' concept of poetry built up on purely individual—psychological foundation is hardly acceptable to Eliot. Eliot eloquently writes: "Mr. Richards like every serious critic of poetry, is a serious moralist as well. His ethics, or theory of value, is one which I cannot accept; or rather, I cannot accept any such theory which is created upon purely individual—psychological foundations."[14] Clarifying his concept of poetry Eliot further says that the function of poetry is not merely to select or reject but organize. A classroom-interpretation of poetry based on verbal and structural pattern, says Eliot, lacks reorganization. Thus, Eliot applies a moral, logical and comprehensive approach of interpreting poetry which bears close resemblance to that of Pound's precision, accuracy and clarity. He identifies the psychological and sociological forms of modern criticism. Hence, study of criticism, says Eliot, is not limited to "a sequence of random conjectures, but as a re-adaptation, may also help us to draw some conclusions as to what is permanent or eternal in poetry, and what is merely the expression of the spirit of an age, and by discovering what does change, how, and why, we may become able to apprehend what does not change".[15]

As Eliot was inspired by Matthew Arnold, he strikes a note between culture and anarchy. Eliot's cultural outlook is twofold. First that assimilating cultures give rise to ethnological confusion; secondly he argues for setting right the ethnological confusion caused by the prevalence of assimilating cultures—also becomes evident from his plays. In *The Cocktail Party*, Eliot highlights the problem of assimilation of cultures; consequences and after effects. In *The Family Reunion*, characters come out of the cross-cultural stock of society; they interact, argue and look around in order to assert their cross-cultural identity. Eliot himself makes confession of the basic fact how every generation has its own proclivity, preference and response to art, culture and society. From this standpoint, Eliot significantly writes:

> Being a period of rapid assimilation; the end may not know the beginning, so different may the taste become.[16]

Ransom finds Eliot's poetry too much psychologistic and less cognitive in treatment and applicability. To Vyvor Winters Eliot is a poet of automation Winters, not only analyzed but also classified poetic structures whereas Cleanth Brooks contributed by close textual analysis. The age of poetry, says T.S. Eliot, is also the age of poetry.[17] From Pound's point of view poetry with all its accuracy and clarity is modelled to impart a social function. It was this perspective by virtue of which Pound redrafted *The Wasteland* in his own image. He redrafted *The Wasteland* in consonance of the definition of poetry given by him that poetry is something akin to inspired mathematics. Eliot on the other hand invented a new form of poetry which adjusts and accommodates assimilating identities. The new function of poetry as discerned by Eliot in the post-modern context is how poetry to him is a melting pot of identities. Eliot stands close to Pound. Poetry to Pound is as simple as good prose: it is something like inspired mathematics depicting human relationship with utmost accuracy and perfection. Poetry to W.B. Yeats is truth seen with passion. The series of images felicitated to form objective co-relative is a means not an end in itself rather a technique applied by Eliot is to adjust, assimilate and even reorganize various modes of heterogeneous experiences. To T.S. Eliot, poetry from the cross-cultural perspective, is a melting pot of identities performing and imparting a social function in the post-modern context. Interpreting Eliot's poetry as the poetry of rootlessness, spiritual sterility and alienation, simply illustrates a partial interpatation of Eliot's poetry from the literal standpoint. Therefore, the cross-cultural identity emanating from assimilation of identities and cultures, at length, projects the whole gamut of the new emerging consciousness and behavior.

NOTES

1. Jawaharlal Nehru, *India's Freedom*, Unwin Books, London, ed. 1962, p. 67.
2. *Ibid.*
3. T.S. Eliot, *Selected Poems*, *The Fire Sermon*, ed.; 1980, p. 58.
4. G.K. Chesterton, "On Carlyle's Past and Present", several essays edited by G.I.J. Cumberledge Oxford University Press, ed. 1952.
5. T.S. Eliot, "What The Thunder Said", *Selected Poems*, p. 65.
6. T.S. Eliot, "Marina, Selected Poems", p. 104.
7. T.S. Eliot, "Ash-Wednesday", *Selected Poems*, p. 90.
8. *Essays of Aldous Huxley*: Selected and edited by S.K. Kumar, Macmillan Indian Ltd., ed., 1988, p. 177.
9. *Ibid.*, p. 178.
10. T.S. Eliot, *The Use of Poetry and the Use of Criticism*, Faber and Faber, London, p. 177.
11. *Ibid.*
12. *Ibid.*
13. *Ibid.*, p. 18.
14. *Ibid.*, p. 17.
15. *Ibid.*, p. 27.
16. *Ibid.*, p. 33.
17. *Ibid.*, p. 30.

Bibliography

By T.S. Eliot

Selected Poems, Faber & Faber, London, ed. 1980.

Four Quartets.

After Strange Gods, London Faber & Faber, ed. 1934.

The Use of Poetry and the Use of Criticism, Faber & Faber, ed. 1933.

Three Essays, Edited by Shiv K. Kumar.

The Cocktail Party, Faber & Faber, ed. 1971.

The Family Reunion. Introduction and Notes by Nevin Coghill, Published by R. Dayal, Oxford University Press, New Delhi, ed., 1948.

Notes Towards the Definition of Culture, London, Faber & Faber, ed. 1948.

The Idea of a Christian Society; Faber & Faber, London, ed. 1939.

Selected Essays: 1917-1932, Brace & Co., New York, Harcourt, 1950.

Murder in the Cathedral.

Introducing James Joyce.

A Choice of Kipling's Verse, Selected by T.S. Eliot, Faber and Faber

Old Possum's Book of Practical Cats.

On Poetry and Poets; New Harcourt, Brace & Co., 1956.

The Sacred Wood: Essays on Poetry and Criticism; London: Methuen & Co., Ltd., ed., 1920.

For Lancet Andrews: *Essays on Style and Order*; London: Faber & Gwyer, 1928.

The Music of Poetry; Glasgow, Jackson, ed., 1942.

On T.S. Eliot

A Book of Poems: An Anthology of English Verse, Edited & Annotated by S.K. Prasad and J.P. Singh, National Delhi, ed. 1973.

American Poetry: An Introductory Anthology, edited by Donald Hall, Faber & Faber, ed. 1969.

Auden, W.H., *Selected Poems*, Faber & Faber.

Baker, Charles, Hemingway, Princeton, New Jersey, Princeton University Press, ed. 1972.

Bhushan, Bharat, *Principles of Literary Criticism* (Plato to T.S. Eliot), Malviya Prakashan, ed. 1959.

Carlyle, Thomas, *Past & Present, Everyman's Library*, London, ed. 1962.

Cassirer, Ernest, *An Essay on Man*, London, Yale University Press, ed. 1969.

Conard, Joseph, *The Heart of Darkness*, Surjeet Publications, New Delhi, ed. 1988.

Critics on Yeats; edited by Raymond Cowell, Universal Book Stall, ed. 1992.

Davie Donald, *Pound Fontana*, Collins, ed. 1975.

Engels, Fredrick, *A Biography*, Translated into English, Progress Publishing, ed. 1974.

Essays of Aldous Huxley, Selected and edited by S.K. Kumar, Macmillan India Ltd., Madras, ed. 1988.

Evance, Ifor, *Short History of English Literature*, Penguin Books, ed. 1990.

Faith of a Historian, Selection from Arnold Toynbee. General edition. K.M. Munshi, R.R. Diwakar, Bhartiya Vidya Bhawan, Library, ed. 1967.

Forster, E.M., *Aspects of the Novel*, Penguin Books, ed. 1974.

Gardner, Helen, *The Art of T.S. Eliot*, ed. 1949.

Gilli, Christopher, *Movements in English Literature (1900-1940)*, Cambridge University Press, ed. 1975.

Goodman, W.R., *Quintessence of Literary Essays*, Doaba House, Nai Sarak, ed. 1980.

Heller, Joseph, *Catch* 22.

Images of Life: An Anthology of Poems, edited by Neil O'Brien, Frank Bros & Co., ed. 1999.

Jha, B.K., *Modern English Classical Poetry*, Mittal Publications, New Delhi, ed. 1996.

Johnson, Samuel, *Lives of the English Poets*, with an Introduction by John Wain, Universal Book Stall, New Delhi, ed. 1992.

Jung, C.G., *Memories, Dreams, Reflections*, The Fountana Library, Collins, ed. 1973.

Kenner, H., *The Invisible Poet, T.S. Eliot*, 1960.

Laski, Harold, *The Rise of European Liberalism*, London, Unwin Book, ed. 1962.

Lu, Fei-Pai, *The Dialectical Structure of the Theory of Poetry*, University of Chicago, ed. 1966.

Michael, Reck, *Ezra Pound*, Rupert Hart-Davis Ltd., London, ed. 1967.

Naipaul, V.S., *The Sufferage of Elvira*, Penguin Books, ed. 1982.

Nehru, Jawaharlal, *Glimpses of the World History*.

Nehru, Jawaharlal, *India's Freedom*, Unwin Books, London, ed. 1936.

Nehru, Jawaharlal, *Nehru's Letters to His Daughter*, Bhartiya Parkashan, Patna.

Nehru, Jawaharlal, *The Discovery of India*.

Notes of Literature; T.S. Eliot, by John Press, No. 83, The British Council.

Persad, *A Background to the Study of English Literature*, Macmillan, Revised edition, ed. 1999.

Plath Sylvia, *Aeriel*, Faber & Faber, London.

Poetry of the 1940s, an Anthology Selected & Edited by Howard Sergeant, Longman, ed. 1970.

Pound, Ezra, *Selected Cantos*, Faber & Faber, London.

Pound, Ezra, *Selected Poems* (1909-1965), Faber & Faber Ltd., London, edited with an introduction by William Cookson, ed. 1973.

Rahman, A., *George Orwell: A Humanistic Perspective*, Atlantic Publishers, ed. 2002.

Rahman, A., *Dialectics of Freedom in Somerset Maugham*, Kalpaz Publishers, Pvt. Ltd., New Delhi, ed. 2005.

Rajaram, Kalpana; *Facets of Indian Culture*, Revised edition, Spectrum India, ed. 1994.

Richards, I.A., *Principles of Literary Criticism*, Universal Book Stall, New Delhi, ed. 2002.

Russell Bertrand, *On Education*, Unwin Books, London, ed. 1960.

Russell, Bertrand, *Has a Man Future?* George Allen & Unwin Books, ed. 1961.

Sahni, C.L., *Matthew Arnold*, Literary Publication, Bureau, Bareilly, ed. 1962.

Snow, C.P., *The Two Cultures, Aspects of English Prose*, Selected and Edited by K.M. Tiwary. RCP Sinha, Vikas Publishing House, Pvt. Ltd., ed. 1988.

Southam B.C., *A Student's Guide to Poems of T.S. Eliot*, Faber & Faber, ed. 1968.

Spender, Stephen, *Selected Poems*, Faber Faber.

The New Oxford Book of American Verse; Chosen and edited by Richard Ellmann New York, Oxford University Press, ed. 1976.

The Pelican Guide to English Literature, The Modern Age edited by Boris Ford, ed. 1970.

The Translations of Ezra Pound; with Introduction by Hugh Kenner, Faber & Faber, ed. 1970.

The Winged Word: An Anthology of Poems for degree course edited by David Green, The Macmillan Co., India Ltd., Calcutta, ed. 1974.

Thoreau, Henry David, *American Thinkers Series*.

Thorp William, *American Writing in the 20th Century*, Harvard University Press, Cambridge, ed. 1963.

Toynbee, Arnold, *Greek Civilization and Character*, A Menter Book, ed. 1953.

Vivas, Eliseo, *Objective Correlative* and *T.S. Eliot*, American Bookman, ed. 1944.

Watson, George, *The Literary Critics*, Penguin Books, ed. 1964.

Watson, George, "The Triumph of Eliot", *Critical Quarterly Winter*, ed. 1965.

William K. Wimsatt Jr., and Cleanth Brooks, *Literary Criticism: A Short History*, Oxford & IBH Publishing Co. Pvt. Ltd., New Delhi, ed. 1957.

Williamson, G., *A Reader's Guide to T.S. Eliot*, New York, ed. 1953.

Winters, Yvor, Eliot: "The Illusion of Reaction", Kenyan, *Review Winter*, ed. 1941.

Wolleim, Richard, *Art and the Objects*; Cambridge University Press, ed. 1992.

Yeats, W.B., *Selected Poetry*, Edited by A. Norman Jeffares, Radha Publishing House, Calcutta.

Index

A Passage to India, 71, 116
Aaesthetic Beauty, 24
Achebe, Chinua, 5, 56
African Literature, 40
After Strange Gods, 50, 77, 98, 112
Alder, 111
Algebra of Infinities, 110
Ambiguity, 14, 21-22, 31, 51, 53, 112
Ambivalence, 3, 37-38, 51, 108, 112
American Tradition, 2, 14-15, 37, 103
Among School Children, 31, 84
Anachronism, 12
Animal Farm, 18, 110
Archetypal, 10, 21, 95, 99,
Arnold, Matthew, 4-5, 30, 49, 55, 75, 78-79, 88, 112, 117-18
Art and Morality, 63, 74-76, 96
Art for Art's Sake, 113
Ash Wednesday, 37-39, 60, 82, 88-90, 104, 109, 114
Aspects of the Novel, 112
Assimilation of Identities, 6, 16, 34, 43-44, 47, 92, 119
Auden, W., 121
Austen, Jane, 111
Austro Hungarian Aristocracy, 40

Baudlair, 2, 12, 22, 24, 37, 50,
Beardsley, 10
Behavioural patterns, 101
Boston, 54, 64, 78, 104, 109
Bradley, F.H., 2, 37, 52
Bradley, Monore C., 10
British Isles, 5, 39, 104, 109
British Tradition, 1, 15-16, 103
Britisher's Eye, 5
Brooks, Cleanth, 7, 11, 21-22, 118
Buckley, Vincent, 51, 112
Burial of the Dead, 40, 90, 96
Burnt Norton, 82-84
Byrant, William Cullen, 85

Canadian Literature, 40
Carlyle, Thomas, 121
Catch 22, 71, 122
Caudwell, Christopher, 6, 8, 42, 74, 77, 93, 113
Celtic Culture, 29, 31-32, 93
Celtic Movement, 29
Chaucer, 47, 89, 106-107
Chaucerian Era, 106
Chaudhuri, Nirad C., 95
Chesterton, G.K., 108, 119
Christian framework, 87
Clash-Culture, 4, 17, 55, 91, 113
Coleridge, S.T., 24, 39
Common Pursuit, 53, 62, 70
Conrad, Joseph, 5, 56, 111
Corbiere, Tristan, 26
Cosmospolitanism, 116
Cross Cultural Behaviour, 5, 56
Cross Cultural Identity, 5, 65, 67, 101, 118-19
Cross Cultural Perspective, 5, 53, 55-56, 80, 88, 91-92, 116
Cuchulain, 29, 32
Culture Shock, 4, 91, 113

Damyata, 80, 114
Dante, 2, 37, 49, 51, 85
Das, Kamla, 87
Datta, 80, 114
Dayadhavam, 80, 114
Death by Water, 96
Deserted Village, 91
Dickinson, Emily, 54, 87
Disillusionment, 28, 64, 83
Dissociation of Sensibility, 3, 15, 35, 47, 50, 94, 104, 107
Dry Salvages, 79, 84

East Coker, 82-83
Ellmann, Richard, 86, 99-100, 102, 123
Emerson, 85
Empson, William, 7, 10-11, 20-21, 88
Engels, 74-75, 121
Enigma of Arrival, 41, 109
European Civilization, 96, 100, 116

Fancy, 25, 39, 100
Fantasy, 100
Fechner, 25
Feminist, 87-88
Fire Sermon, 83, 90, 119
Flaubert, 3, 34, 41, 49, 85, 104
Forster, E.M., 17, 44, 70-71, 79, 91, 95, 99, 116
Four Quartets, 37, 39, 80-81, 83-84, 100, 104, 109, 111, 114
French Symbolists, 22
From Ritual to Romance, 8
Frontiers of Criticism, 8, 22, 41, 55, 117
Frost, Robert, 1, 103

Gandhi, M.K., 100
Gingberg, Allen, 97
Gomme, Andor, 80
Gourmont, Remy de, 87

Graves, Robert, 10-11, 20
Gray, Thomas, 107
Great Tradition, 53, 58, 62, 70, 111
Greene, Graham, 5, 56

Hanarhan, 29, 32
Heller, Joseph, 122
Hemingway, Earnest, 54, 94
Historical Criticism, 10, 21
Historical perspective, 10-11
Hoggart, Richard, 96
Hollow Men, 5, 40-41, 47-48, 65, 78, 107
Homage to Sextus Properties, 72
Hugh Selwyn Mauberley, 24, 72
Hulme, 22-23, 25, 50
Humanistic Movement, 2
Huxley, Aldous, 97-98, 115

Ideograph, 4, 23, 25, 108, 115-17
Immediate Experience, 2-3, 36, 52, 104
Indian Culture and Civilization, 100
Indian Mythology, 34, 80-81, 90-91, 113
Instigations, 23

Jacobean Age, 78
James, Henry, 24
Jung, 7, 81, 111

Kafka, 67
Keynes, 71
Kipling, 116, 120
Kyd, 95

Laforgue, 2, 16, 26, 37, 47, 49, 76
Lawrence, D.H., 18, 41, 53, 76, 96
Leavis, 4, 7-11, 13, 20, 35, 41-42, 49, 51, 53, 55, 61-64, 70, 88-89, 96, 99, 108, 111-12, 115
Leda and the Swan, 32
Lewis, Day, 6, 28
Lucas, F.L., 111

Macneice, 28, 85
Magnetic Mountain, 6
Mallarme, 22, 24
Mandela, 111
Marina, 109, 114
Marx, Karl, 74, 76
Marxists, 99
Mass Civilization, 99
Mauberley Poems, 116
Maugham, Somerset, 21, 84
Meaning of Meaning, 21-22
Miller, Arthur, 54, 94
Minority Culture, 99
Mississippi, 79
Modus Operandi, 13, 101
Monroe, Harriet, 25, 108
Multi Culturalisism, 71, 88
Murder in Cathedral, 92
Murry, Middleton, 52, 81
Mythical, 11

Naipaul, V.S., 5, 17, 38-41, 44-46, 70-71, 100, 108-09
Naturalism, 47
Naturalists, 27, 35
Nehru, Jawaharlal, 105

New Apocalypse, 12
New Bearings in Poetry, 62
New Criticism, 3, 7, 9-11, 14, 19-21, 53, 111
New Critics, 3, 7-11, 14, 19-21, 24, 41-42, 58, 88, 111
New Oxford Book, 100, 101-102, 123
Notes Towards the Definition of Culture, 35, 77, 96
Nymphs, 107

Objective Correlative, 26, 49
Odgen, 7
Old India, 80
Old Testament, 12
Orwell, George, 18, 54, 76, 85, 110
Owen, Wilfred, 85

Paradox, 9, 14, 39, 67
Pater, Walter, 85, 113
Pathetic Fallacy, 18, 106, 110
Pessimism, 18, 37, 78, 104, 110, 113-14
Philosophy of Rhetorics, 22-23
Phoenician Sailor, 99
Plath, Sylvia, 54, 87, 97
Poetry and Morality, 51, 112
Portrait of a Lady, 15, 46, 48, 60, 116
Post Modern, 5, 17-18, 56, 88, 110, 119
Post-War Europe, 40, 88, 90, 97
Pound, Ezra, 4, 8, 17, 24, 32, 41, 46, 49-50, 72, 81-82, 85, 103, 112, 115-16
Practical Criticism, 56, 111
Principles of Literary Criticism, 21, 23
Proletariat, 27, 74, 75, 113
Psycho-Analysis, 25

Rainbow, 18
Ransom, 26, 118
Razor's Edge, 84-85
Read, Herbert, 14, 53
Realism, 47, 58, 103
Rhythm, 1, 12, 16, 22-23, 25, 70-71, 79, 86-87, 100, 108
Richards, I.A., 7, 9, 11, 13, 20, 23, 25-26, 35, 50, 58, 66, 83, 88-90, 94, 104, 106, 111, 116
Russell, Bertrand, 72, 100

Sailing to Byzantium, 28-30
Salinger, 77, 97
Sampson, George, 70, 78, 86, 97, 99, 101
Second Coming, 29, 31, 32, 88
Selected Essays, 26, 51, 112
Semantic Principle, 21, 23, 111
Seven Types of Ambiguities, 7, 21
Shakespeare, 26, 30, 51
Shaw, G.B., 27, 54, 75, 77, 89
Smith, Gold, 103
Snow, 95, 98, 101, 123
Sociological Perspective, 9, 42
Sons and Lovers, 53, 76
Spender, Stephen, 9, 27-28, 42, 76, 93, 99
Sphinx, 29
Spiritus Mundi, 30-31, 38

St. Augustine, 91

Summing Up, 21

Syllogism, 21-22

Synaesthesia, 23

Syntactical, 24

Tagore, 91

Tate, Allen, 11, 52

Tennyson, 50

Thames, 40, 83, 97, 107

The Canterbury Tales, 47, 89, 107

The Cocktail Party, 16, 47-48, 60, 67-68, 92, 118

The Divine Comedy, 49, 85

The Family Reunion, 39, 68-69, 92, 100, 118

The Idea of a Christian Society, 98, 112

Thomas, Dylan, 12

Thoreau, 103

Thoughts After Lambeth, 50, 98

"Tradition and the Individual Talent", 13, 35, 43, 45, 51, 59, 61-62, 66, 81, 96, 115

Transcendence, 2, 18, 37, 70, 104, 110

Unified Sensibility, 70, 94, 113-114

Upanishad, 80, 91

Urbanization, 1, 4, 35, 91

Utopia, 75

Victorian Era, 30, 116

Wasteland, 4, 12, 24, 28, 35, 37, 40-41, 43, 46-51, 59, 76, 78, 80, 83, 85-86, 89-90, 94, 96, 98-99, 101, 104, 107, 110, 112, 115, 117,

Western Civilization, 100

Weston, Jessie, 90

What the Thunder Said, 91, 119

White Man's Burden, 116

Whitman, 85

Wilde, Oscar, 34, 85

Williams, 85-86, 124

Wilson, Edmund, 52, 111

Wimsatt Jr., W.K., 10, 22

Winters, Vyvor, 26

Women in Love, 18, 24, 53

Woolf, Virginia, 20, 22, 87,

Wordsworth, 52, 79, 81

Wright, Richard, 5, 56

Yeats W.B., 28, 38, 45, 47, 50, 84, 88, 119

Yogi and the Commissar, 85